LogicNotes
with
Practice Problems

Samuel H. LiPuma
Cuyahoga Community College

Richard W. Miller
University of Missouri – Rolla

Introduction

to

Logic

Twelfth Edition

Irving M. Copi
University of Hawaii

Carl Cohen
University of Michigan

PEARSON

Prentice
Hall

Upper Saddle River, New Jersey 07458

Copyright © 2005 by Pearson Education, Inc.
Upper Saddle River, New Jersey 07458

Printed in the United States of America

10 9 8 7 6 5 4 3 2 1

ISBN 0-13-191310-7

Table of Contents

Chapter 1: Basic Logical Concepts
Key Terms

Argument	A structured group of propositions, organized to support an inference.
Classical Logic	Traditional techniques, based on Aristotle's works, for determining whether deductive arguments are valid.
Compound Proposition	A proposition made up of two or more simple propositions.
Conclusion	The proposition in an argument that the other propositions, taken together, all support.
Deductive Argument	Claims to support its conclusion conclusively; one of the two classes of argument.
Disjunctive (or Alternative) Proposition	A type of compound proposition; either component could be false.
Hypothetical (or Conditional) Proposition	A type of compound proposition; either or both components could be false.
Inductive Argument	Claims to support its conclusion with some degree of probability; one of the two classes of argument.
Inference	A process of linking propositions.
Invalid Argument	The conclusion is not necessarily true, even if all the premises are true; applies only to deductive arguments.
Logic	The study of the methods and principles used to distinguish correct from incorrect reasoning.
Modern Symbolic Logic	Methods used by most modern logicians to determine whether deductive arguments are valid.
Premise	A proposition used in an argument.
Probability	The likelihood (but not certainty) that the premises of an inductive argument support its conclusion.
Proposition	An assertion of what is (or is not) the case; all propositions are either true or false.

Simple Proposition	A proposition having only one part.
Sound	An argument that is valid and has only true premises.
Statement	The meaning of a declarative sentence at a particular time; in log the word "statement" is sometimes used instead of "proposition."
Truth	An attribute of a proposition, asserting what is really the case.
Valid Argument	If all the premises are true, the conclusion must be true; applies only to deductive arguments.

Chapter 1: Basic Logical Concepts

1.1 What Logic Is

1.2 Propositions

1.3 Arguments

1.4 Deductive and Inductive Arguments

1.5 Validity and Truth

I. Some *valid* arguments contain *only true propositions*- true premises and a true conclusion

II. Some *valid* arguments contain *only false* propositions

III. Some *invalid* arguments contain *only true propositions*- all their premises are true, and their conclusions are true as well

IV. Some *invalid* arguments contain *only true premises* and have a *false conclusion*

V. Some *valid* arguments have *false premises* and a *true conclusion*

VI. Some *invalid* arguments also have *false premises* and a *true conclusion*

VII. Some *invalid* arguments, of course, contain *all false propositions*- false premises and a false conclusion

Chapter 2: Analyzing Arguments
Key Terms

Command

A directive statement.

Conclusion-Indicator

A word or phrase that typically introduces an argument's conclusion.

Enthymeme

An argument containing an unstated proposition.

Explanation

A group of statements accounting for why something is the way it is; an explanation is not an argument.

Premise-Indicator

A word or phrase that typically introduces a premise in an argument.

Rhetorical Question

A question whose answer is assumed to be obvious.

Chapter 2: Analyzing Arguments

2.1 Paraphrasing and Diagramming

Paraphrasing

Diagramming

Interwoven arguments

2.2 Recognizing Arguments

Conclusion-Indicators and Premise-Indicators

Premises not in Declarative Form

Unstated Propositions

2.3 Arguments and Explanations

2.4 Complex Argumentative Passages

2.5 Problems in Reasoning

Chapter 3: The Uses of Language
Key Terms

Ceremonial Use of Language   A mix of languages (usually expressive and directive) with special social uses.

Directive Discourse   Language used to cause or prevent specific action.

Expressive Discourse   Language used to convey or evoke feelings.

Informative Discourse   Language used to convey information.

Performative Utterance   A special form of speech that simultaneously reports on, and performs some function.

Chapter 3: The Uses of Language

3.1 The Basic Functions of Language

3.2 Discourse Serving Multiple Functions

3.3 Language Forms and Language Functions

3.4 Emotive and Neutral Language

3.5 Agreement and Disagreement in Attitude and Belief

Chapter 4: Definition
Key Terms

Ambiguity

Uncertainty because a word or phrase has more than one meaning.

Circular Definition

A faulty definition; the definition relies on knowledge of what is being defined.

Conventional Intension

The commonly accepted intension; the public meaning that does not require omniscience.

Criterial Dispute

A form of genuine dispute that at first appears to be merely verbal.

Definiendum

The symbol being defined.

Definiens

The symbol (or group of symbols) that has the same meaning as the definiendum.

Definition by Genus and Difference

Using a combination of shared class attributes (genus) and specific distinguishing attributes (difference) to specify definition.

Extension

The collection of objects to which a general term can be applied.

Intension

The attributes shared by all objects, and only those objects, to which a general term applies.

Lexical Definition

A report – which may be true or false – of the meaning a definiendum already has in actual language usage.

Objective Intension

The total set of attributes shared by all objects in the word's extension, which would require omniscience to understand.

Operational Definition

Defining a term by limiting its use to situations where certain actions or operations lead to specified results.

Ostensive Definition

A demonstrative definition; a term is defined by pointing at an object.

Persuasive Definition	A definition intended to influence attitudes or stir emotions.
Precising Definition	A report on existing language usage, with additional stipulations provided to reduce vagueness.
Quasi-Ostensive Definition	A denotative definition that uses gesture and a descriptive phrase.
Stipulative Definition	A proposal to arbitrarily assign meaning to a newly introduced symbol.
Subjective Intension	What the speaker believes is the intension; the private interpretation at a particular time.
Synonymous Definition	Defining a word with another word that has the same meaning and is already understood.
Theoretical Definition	An attempt to create a description that is useful in theoretical exploration or in scientific practice.
Vagueness	Lack of clarity regarding the 'borders' of a term's meaning.

Chapter 4: Definition

4.1 Disputes and Definitions

4.2 Definitions and Their Uses

Stipulative Definitions

Lexical Definitions

Precising Definitions

Theoretical Definitions

Persuasive Definitions

4.3 Extension, Intension and the Structure of Definitions

16

4.4 Extension and Denotative Definitions

4.5 Intension and Intensional Definition

4.6 Rules for Definition by Genus and Difference

Rule 1: A definition should state the essential attributes of the species

Rule 2: A definition must not be circular

Rule 3: A definition must be neither too broad nor too narrow

Rule 4: Ambiguous, obscure, or figurative language must not be used in a definition

Rule 5: A definition should not be negative where it can be affirmative

Chapter 5: Fallacies
Key Terms

Accent	A fallacy in which a phrase is used to convey two different meanings within an argument, and the difference is based on changes in emphasis given to words within the phrase.
Accident	A fallacy in which a generalization is wrongly applied to a particular case.
Amphiboly	A fallacy in which a loose or awkward combination of words can be interpreted more than one way; the argument contains a premise based on the true interpretation, but the conclusion relies on a false interpretation.
Appeal to Emotion	A fallacy in which the argument relies on emotion rather than reason. Also known as argument ad populum.
Appeal to Force	A fallacy in which the argument relies on the threat of force; the threat may be veiled. Also known as argument ad baculum.
Appeal to Inappropriate Authority	A fallacy in which a conclusion is based on the judgment of an "authority" who has no legitimate claim to expertise in the matter. Also known as argument ad verecundiam.
Appeal to Pity	A fallacy in which the argument relies on generosity, altruism, and mercy, rather than reason. Also known as argument ad misericordiam.
Argument ad hominem	A fallacy in which the argument relies on an attack against the person taking a position; an ad hominem attack can be abusive, or circumstantial.
Argument from Ignorance	A fallacy in which a proposition is held to be true just because it has not been proved false, or false just because it has not been proved true. Also known as argument ad ignorantium.

Begging the Question	A fallacy in which the conclusion is stated or assumed within one of the premises. Also known as petitio principii or as a circular argument.
Complex Question	A fallacy in which a question is asked in a way that presupposes the truth of a conclusion buried within the question.
Composition	A fallacy in which an inference is mistakenly drawn from the attributes of the parts of a whole, to the attributes of the whole.
Division	A fallacy in which a mistaken inference is drawn from the attributes of a whole to the attributes of the parts of the whole.
Equivocation	A fallacy in which two or more meanings of a word or phrase are used in different parts of an argument.
Fallacy	A type of argument that may seem to be correct, but contains a mistake in reasoning.
Fallacy of Ambiguity	A type of fallacy caused by a shift or confusion of meanings within an argument. Also known as a sophism.
Fallacy of Defective Induction	A fallacy in which the premises are too weak or ineffective to warrant the conclusion.
Fallacy of Presumption	A fallacy in which the conclusion depends on a tacit assumption that is dubious, unwarranted, or false.
Fallacy of Relevance	A fallacy in which the premises are irrelevant to the conclusion.
False Cause	A fallacy in which something that is not really a cause, is treated as a cause. Also known as non causa pro causa.
Hasty Generalization	A fallacy in which one moves carelessly from individual cases to generalization. Also known as converse accident.

Irrelevant Conclusion	A type of fallacy in which the premises support a different conclusion than the one that is proposed. Also known as ignoratio elenchi.
Non Sequitor	"Does not follow"; often applied to fallacies of relevance, since the conclusion does not follow from the premises.
Poisoning the Well	A type of ad hominem attack that cuts off rational discourse.
Post Hoc Ergo Propter Hoc	"After the thing, therefore because of the thing"; a type of false cause fallacy in which an event is presumed to have been caused by another event that came before.
Red Herring Fallacy	A type of irrelevant conclusion fallacy in which a distracting element is added to an opponent's position.
Slippery Slope	A type of false cause fallacy in which change in a particular direction is assumed to lead inevitably to further, disastrous, change in the same direction.
Straw Man Fallacy	A type of irrelevant conclusion fallacy in which the opponent's position is mis-represented.

Chapter 5: Fallacies

5.1 What is a Fallacy?

5.2 The Classifications of Fallacies

5.3 Fallacies of Relevance

R1. The Appeal to Emotion

R2. The Appeal to Pity

R3. The Appeal to Force

R4. The Argument ad hominem

A. *Argument ad hominem, Abusive*

B. *Argument ad hominem, Circumstantial*

R5. Irrelevant Conclusion

5.4 Fallacies of Defective Induction

D1. The Argument from Ignorance

D2. The Appeal to Inappropriate Authority

D3. False Cause

D4. Hasty Generalization

5.5 Fallacies of Presumption

P1. Accident

P2. Complex Question

P3. Begging the Question

5.6 Fallacies of Ambiguity

A1. Equivocation

A2. Amphiboly

A3. Accent

A4. Composition

A5. Division

Chapter 6: Categorical Propositions
Key Terms

Boolean interpretation	The modern interpretation of categorical propositions, in which universal propositions are not assumed to refer to classes that have members.
Categorical Proposition	A proposition that can be used in an argument about the relationship between one category and some other category.
Class	The collection of all objects that have some specified characteristic in common.
Complement of a Class	The collection of all things that do not belong to that class.
Contradictories	Two propositions that cannot both be true and cannot both be false.
Contraposition	An inference formed by replacing the subject term of a proposition with the complement of its predicate term, and replacing the predicate term by the complement of its subject term. Not all contrapositions are valid.
Contraries	Two propositions that cannot both be true; if one is true, the other must be false. They can both be false.
Conversion	An inference formed by interchanging the subject and predicate terms. Not all conversions are valid.
Copula	Any form of the verb "to be" that connects the subject and predicate terms of a categorical proposition.
Deductive Argument	Claims to support its conclusion conclusively; one of the two classes of arguments.
Distribution	A characterization of whether terms in a categorical proposition refer to all members of the class designated by that term.
Existential Fallacy	A fallacy in which the argument relies on the assumption that a class has members, when there is no explicit assertion that it does.

Immediate Inference	An inference drawn directly from only one premise.
Mediate Inference	An inference drawn from more than one premise; the conclusion is drawn from the first premise through the mediation of the second.
Obversion	An inference formed by changing the quality of a proposition and replacing the predicate term by its complement. Obversion is valid for any standard-form categorical proposition.
Opposition	Any logical relation among the kinds of categorical propositions (A, E, I and O) exhibited on the square of opposition.
Particular Affirmative Propositions ("I" Propositions)	Propositions that assert that two classes have some member or members in common; Some S is P.
Particular Negative Propositions ("O" Propositions)	Propositions that assert that at least one member of a class is excluded from another class; Some S is not P.
Quality	An attribute of every categorical proposition, determined by whether the proposition affirms or denies some form of class inclusion.
Quantity	An attribute of every categorical proposition, determined by whether the proposition refers to all members ("universal") or only some members ("particular") of the subject-class.
Square of Opposition	A diagram showing the logical relationships among the four types of categorical propositions (A, E, I and O). The traditional Square of Opposition differs from the modern Square of Opposition in important ways.
Subalternation	The opposition between a universal proposition and its corresponding particular proposition. In classical logic, the universal proposition implies the truth of the particular proposition.
Subcontraries	Two propositions that cannot both be false; they can both be true.
Universal Affirmative Propositions ("A" Propositions)	Propositions that assert that the whole of one class is included or contained in another class; All S is P.

Universal Negative Propositions ("E" Propositions)	Propositions that assert that the whole of one class is excluded from another class; No S is P.
Valid Argument	If all the premises are true, the conclusion must be true.
Venn Diagram	A representation of classes and categorical propositions using overlapping circles.

Chapter 6: Categorical Propositions

6.1 The Theory of Deduction

6.2 Classes and Categorical Propositions

6.3 The Four Kinds of Categorical Propositions

1. Universal affirmative propositions

2. Universal negative propositions

3. Particular affirmative propositions

4. Particular negative propositions

6.4 Quality, Quantity and Distribution

A. Quality

B. Quantity

C. General Schema of Standard-Form Categorical Propositions

D. Distribution

6.5 The Traditional Squares of Opposition

A. Contradictories

B. Contraries

C. Subcontraries

D. Subalternation

E. The Square of Opposition

6.6 Further Immediate Inferences

A. Conversion

B. Classes and Class Complements

C. Obversion

D. Contraposition

6.7 Existential Import and the Interpretation of Categorical Propositions

6.8 Symbolism and Diagrams for Categorical Propositions

Chapter 7: Categorical Syllogisms
Key Terms

Categorical Syllogism	A deductive argument consisting of three categorical propositions that together contain exactly three terms, each of which occurs in exactly two of the constituent propositions.
Existential Fallacy	As a formal fallacy, the mistake of inferring a particular conclusion from two universal premises.
Fallacy of an Illicit Major	A formal mistake in which the major term of a syllogism is undistributed in the major premise, but is distributed in the conclusion.
Fallacy of an Illicit Minor	A formal mistake in which the minor term of a syllogism is undistributed in the minor premise, but is distributed in the conclusion.
Fallacy of Drawing an Affirmative Conclusion from a Negative Premise	A formal mistake in which one premise of a syllogism is negative, but the conclusion is affirmative.
Fallacy of Exclusive Premises	A formal mistake in which both premises of a syllogism are negative.
Fallacy of Four Terms	A formal mistake in which a categorical syllogism contains more than three terms.
Fallacy of the Undistributed Middle	A formal mistake in which a categorical syllogism contains a middle term that is not distributed in either premise.
Figure	The logical shape of a syllogism, determined by the position of the middle term in its premises; there are four possible figures.
Major Term/Major Premise	The term that occurs as the predicate of the conclusion in a standard-form syllogism. The premise containing the major term is the major premise.
Middle Term	The term that occurs in both propositions, but never in the conclusion, of a standard-form syllogism.
Minor Term/Minor Premise	The term that occurs as the subject of the conclusion in a standard-form syllogism. The premise containing the minor term is the minor premise.

Mood	One of the 64 characterizations of categorical syllogisms determined by the forms of the standard-form propositions it contains.
Standard-form Categorical Syllogism	A categorical syllogism in which the premises and conclusions are all standard-form categorical propositions (A,E, I or O) and are arranged with the major premise first, minor premise second, and conclusion last.
Syllogism	Any deductive argument in which a conclusion is inferred from two premises.

Chapter 7: Categorical Syllogisms

7.1 Standard-Form Categorical Syllogisms

A. Terms of s Syllogism: Major, Minor and Middle.

B. The Mood of the Syllogism

C. The Figure of the Syllogism

7.2 The Formal Nature of Syllogistic Argument

7.3 Venn Diagram Technique for Testing Syllogisms

7.4 Syllogistic Rules and Syllogistic Fallacies

Rule 1. Avoid four terms

Rule 2. Distribute the middle terms in at least one premise

Rule 3. Any term distributed in the conclusion must be distributed in the premises

Rule 4. Avoid two negative premises

Rule 5. If either premise is negative, the conclusion must be negative

Rule 6. From two universal premises no particular conclusion may be drawn

7.5 Exposition of the 15 Valid forms of the Categorical Syllogism

7.6 Deduction of the 15 Valid Forms of the Categorical Syllogism

7.7 Deduction of the 15 Valid Forms of the Categorical Syllogism

Case1. If the conclusion of the syllogism is an A proposition

Case 2. If the conclusion of the syllogism is an E proposition

Case 3. If the conclusion is an I proposition

Case 4. If the conclusion is an O proposition

Chapter 8: Syllogisms in Ordinary Language
Key Terms

Dilemma

A common form of argument in ordinary discourse in which it is claimed that a choice must be made between two (usually bad) alternatives.

Disjunctive Syllogism

A form of argument in which one premise is a disjunction and the conclusion claims the truth of one of the disjuncts. Only some disjunctive syllogisms are valid.

Enthymeme

An argument containing an unstated proposition.

Exceptive Proposition

A proposition making two assertions, that all members of some class -- except for members of one of its subclasses -- are members of some other class.

Exclusive Proposition

A proposition asserting that the predicate applies only to the subject named.

Fallacy of Affirming the Consequent

A formal fallacy in which the categorical premise affirms the consequent, rather than the antecedent, of the conditional premise.

Fallacy of Denying the Antecedent

A formal fallacy in which the categorical premise denies the antecedent, rather than the consequent, of the conditional premise.

First-Order Enthymeme

An incompletely stated argument in which the proposition that is taken for granted is the major premise.

Hypothetical Syllogism

A form of argument containing at least one conditional proposition as a premise. Hypothetical syllogisms can be "pure" (all premises are conditional) or "mixed" (one premise is conditional).

Modus Ponens

A valid syllogism in which the categorical premise affirms the antecedent of the conditional premise, and the conclusion affirms its consequent.

Modus Tollens

A valid syllogism in which the categorical premise denies the consequent of the conditional premise, and the conclusion denies its antecedent.

Parameter	An auxiliary symbol that aids in expressing an assertion in standard form.
Reduction to Standard Form	Reformulation of a syllogistic argument into standard form.
Second-Order Enthymeme	An incompletely stated argument in which the proposition that is taken for granted is the minor premise.
Simple/Complex Dilemma	In a simple dilemma, the conclusion is a single categorical proposition; in a complex dilemma, the conclusion itself is a disjunction.
Singular Proposition	A proposition that asserts that a specific individual belongs (or does not belong) to a particular class.
Sorites	An enthymematic argument in which a conclusion is inferred from any number of premises through a chain of syllogistic inferences.
Syllogistic Argument	An argument that is a standard-form categorical syllogism, or can be formulated as one without any change in meaning.
Syllogistic Argument	An argument that is a standard-form categorical syllogism, or can be formulated as one without any change in meaning.
Third-Order Enthymeme	An incompletely stated argument in which the proposition that is taken for granted is the conclusion.
Uniform Translation	Standardizing expressions into a standard-form syllogistic argument by using parameters or other techniques.
Unit Class	A class with only one member.

Chapter 8: Syllogisms in Ordinary Language

8.1 Syllogistic Arguments

8.2 Reducing the Number of Terms to Three

8.3 Translating Categorical Propositions into Standard Form

I. SINGULAR PROPOSITIONS.

II. CATEGORICAL PROPOSITIONS THAT HAVE ADJECTIVES OR ADJECTIVAL PHRASES AS PREDICATES, RATHER THAN SUBSTANTIVES OF CLASS TERMS.

III. CATEGORICAL PROPOSITIONS WHOSE MAIN VERBS ARE OTHER THAN THE STANDARD-FORM COPULA "TO BE".

IV. STATEMENTS IN WHICH THE STANDARD FORM INGREDIENTS ARE ALL PRESENT BUT NOT ARRANGED IN STANDARD-FORM ORDER.

V. CATEGORICAL PROPOSITIONS WHOSE QUANTITIES ARE INDICATED BY WORDS OTHER THAN THE STANDARD-FORM QUANTIFIERS "ALL," "NO," AND "SOME."

VI. EXCLUSIVE PROPOSITIONS.

VII. CATEGORICAL PROPOSITIONS THAT CONTAIN NO WORDS AT ALL TO INDICATE THE QUANTITY.

VIII. PROPOSITIONS THAT DO NOT RESEMBLE STANDARD-FORM CATEGORICAL PROPOSITIONS AT ALL, BUT CAN BE TRANSLATED INTO STANDARD FORM.

IX. EXCEPTIVE PROPOSITIONS

8.4 Uniform Translation

8.5 Enthymemes

8.6 Sorties

8.7 Disjunctive and Hypothetical Syllogisms

8.8 The Dilemma

Chapter 9: Symbolic Logic
Key Terms

Antecedent

In a conditional statement, the component that immediately follows the "if."

Argument Form

An array of symbols exhibiting logical structure; it contains statement variables but no statements.

Biconditional Statement

A compound statement that asserts that its two component statements have the same truth value, and therefore are materially equivalent.

Compound Statement

A statement that contains another statement as a component.

Conditional Statement Conjunction

A compound statement of the form "If p then q." A truth-functional connective meaning "and," symbolized by the dot.

Consequent

In a conditional statement, the component that immediately follows the "then."

Contingent Statement Form

A statement form that has both true and false substitution instances.

De Morgan's Theorems

Two useful logical equivalences: the negation of the disjunction of two statements is logically equivalent to the conjunction of the negations of the two statements; and, the negation of the conjunction of two statements is logically equivalent to the disjunction of the negations of the two statements.

Disjunction

A truth-functional connective meaning "or"; there is a "weak" (inclusive) sense, symbolized by the wedge (or "vee"), and a "strong" (exclusive) sense.

Disjunctive Syllogism

A valid argument form in which one premise is a disjunction, another premise is the denial of one of the two disjuncts, and the conclusion is the truth of the other disjunct.

Double Negation

An expression of logical equivalence between a symbol and the negation of the negation of that symbol.

Fallacy of Affirming the Consequent	A formal fallacy in which the categorical premise affirms the consequent, rather than the antecedent, of the conditional premise.
Fallacy of Denying the Antecedent	A formal fallacy in which the categorical premise denies the antecedent, rather than the consequent, of the conditional premise.
Horseshoe	A symbol used to represent the common, partial meaning of the "if-then" phrase; also, the symbol used to represent material implication.
Hypothetical Syllogism	A valid argument containing only conditional propositions.
Implication	The relation that holds between the antecedent and the consequent of a true conditional statement. There are different kinds of implication.
Invalid Argument Form	An argument form that has at least one substitution instance with true premises and a false conclusion.
Logically Equivalent	Two statements for which the statement of their material equivalence is a tautology; they are equivalent in meaning, and have the same truth value.
Material Implication	A weak truth-functional relation symbolized by the horseshoe that may connect two statements; the statement "p materially implies q" is true when either p is false, or q is true.
Materially Equivalent	Two statements that are both true, or both false; symbolized by the three-bar sign.
Modus Ponens	A valid argument in which the categorical premise affirms the antecedent of the conditional premise, and the conclusion affirms its consequent.
Modus Tollens	A valid argument in which the categorical premise denies the consequent of the conditional premise, and the conclusion denies its antecedent.
Negation	Denial or contradictory, symbolized by the tilde or curl.
Peirce's Law	A tautological statement of the form.

Principle of Excluded Middle	Every statement is either true or false.
Principle of Identity	If any statement is true, it is true.
Principle of Noncontradiction	No statement can be both true and false.
Punctuation	The parentheses, brackets, and braces used in symbolic language to render a statement unambiguous in meaning.
Refutation by Logical Analogy	Exhibiting the fault of an argument by presenting another, obviously faulty argument with the same form.
Self-Contradictory Statement Form	A statement form that has only false substitution instances; a contradiction.
Simple Statement	A statement that does not contain any other statement as a component.
Specific Form of a Statement	The statement form from which the given statement results when a different simple statement is substituted for each different statement variable.
Specific Form of an Argument	The argument form from which the given argument results when a different simple statement is substituted for each different statement variable.
Statement Form	An array of symbols exhibiting logical structure; it contains statement variables but no statements.
Statement Variable	A letter (lower-case) for which a statement may be substituted.
Substitution Instance of a Statement Form	Any statement that results from the consistent substitution of statements for statement variables.
Substitution Instance of an Argument Form	Any argument that results from the consistent substitution of statements for statement variables.
Tautology	A statement form that has only true substitution instances.

Truth Table	An array on which all possible truth values of arguments are displayed, through the display of all possible combinations of the truth values of the argument's components.
Truth Value	The status of any statement as true, or false.
Truth-Functional Component	Any component of a compound statement whose replacement by another statement having the same truth value would not change the truth value of the compound statement.
Truth-Functional Compound Statement	A compound statement whose truth function is determined by the truth values of its components.
Truth-Functional Connective	Any logical connective (including conjunction, disjunction, material implication and material equivalence) between the components of a truth-functional compound statement.
Valid Argument Form	An argument form that has no substitution instances with true premises and a false conclusion.

Chapter 9: Symbolic Logic

9.1 Modern Logic and Its Symbolic Language

9.2 The Symbols for Conjunction, Negation, and Disjunction

A. Conjunction

B. Negation

C. Disjunction

D. Punctuation

9.3 Conditional Statements and Material Implication

9.4 Argument Forms, and Refutation by Logical Analogy

9.5 The Precise Meaning of "Invalid" and "Valid"

9.6 Testing Argument Validity on Truth Tables

9.7 Some Common Argument Forms

A. Common Valid Forms

Disjunctive Syllogism

Modus Ponens

Modus Tollens

Hypothetical Syllogism

B. Common Invalid Forms

C. Substitution Instances and Specific Forms

9.8 Statement Forms and Material Equivalence

A. Statement Forms and Statements

B. Tautologous, Contradictory, and Contingent Statement Forms

C. Material Equivalence

D. Arguments, Conditional Statements and Tautologies

9.9 Logical Equivalence

9.10 The Three "Laws of Thought"

The principle of identity

The principle of noncontradiction

The principle of the excluded middle

Chapter 10: Methods of Deduction
Key Terms

Elementary Valid Argument

Any one of a set of specified deductive arguments that serves as a rule of inference and can be used to construct a formal proof of validity.

Formal Proof of Validity

A sequence of statements ending with a conclusion in an argument whose validity is proved.

Natural Deduction

A method of proving the validity of a deductive argument by using the rules of inference.

Rule of Replacement

The rule that logically equivalent expressions may replace each other.

Rules of Inference

The rules that permit valid inferences from statements assumed as premises.

Chapter 10: Methods of Deduction

10.1 Formal Proof of Validity

10.2 The Rules of Replacement

10.3 Proof of Validity

10.4 Inconsistency

10.5 Indirect Proof of Validity

10.6 Shorter Truth-Table Technique

Chapter 11: Quantification Theory
Key Terms

Affirmative Singular Proposition

A proposition that asserts that a particular individual has some specified attribute.

Asyllogistic Arguments

Arguments in which one or more propositions is more complicated than a categorical proposition.

Existential Generalization (EG)

A rule of inference that permits the valid inference of the existential quantification of a propositional function from any true substitution instance of that function.

Existential Instantiation (EI)

A rule of inference that permits (with restrictions) the valid inference of the truth of a substitution instance for an individual constant that appears nowhere earlier in the existential quantification of a propositional function.

Existential Quantifier

A symbol (∃x) indicating that the propositional function that follows has some true substitution instance.

Generalization

The process of forming a proposition from a propositional function by placing a universal quantifier or an existential quantifier before it.

Individual Constant

A symbol used in logical notation to denote an individual.

Individual Variable

A symbol used as a placeholder for an individual constant.

Instantiation

The process of forming a proposition from a propositional function by substituting an individual constant for its individual variable.

Normal-Form Formula

A formula in which negation signs apply only to simple predicates.

Propositional Function

An expression that contains an individual variable and becomes a statement when an individual constant is substituted for the individual variable.

Quantification

A method for describing and symbolizing by reference to their inner logical structure.

Simple Predicate

A propositional function having some true and some false substitution instances, each of which is an affirmative singular proposition.

Universal Generalization (UG)

A rule of inference that permits the valid inference of a universally quantified expression from an expression that is given as true of any arbitrarily selected individual.

Universal Instantiation (UI)

A rule of inference that permits the valid inference of any substitution instance of a propositional function from its universal quantification.

Universal Quantifier

A symbol, (x), used before a propositional function to assert that the predicate following is true of everything.

Chapter 11: Quantification Theory

11.1 The Need for Quantification

11.2 Singular Proposition

11.3 The Universal and Existential Quantifiers

11.4 Traditional Subject-Predicate Propositions

11.5 Proving Validity

11.6 Proving Invalidity

11.7 Asyllogistic Inference

Chapter 12: Analogical Reasoning

Analogical Argument

An inductive argument in which it is concluded that two entities, alike in some respect(s), are alike in some other respect.

Analogy

A likeness drawn between two or more entities in one or more respects.

Disanalogy

A point of difference between the cases mentioned in the premises and the case mentioned in the conclusion of an analogical argument.

Refutation by Logical Analogy

Exhibiting the fault of an inductive argument by presenting another, clearly flawed argument with a doubtful conclusion, having essentially the same form.

Chapter 12: Analogical Reasoning

12.1 Induction and Deduction Revisited

12.2 Argument by Analogy

12.3 Appraising Analogical Arguments

I. NUMBER OF ENTITIES

II. VARIETY OF THE INSTANCES IN THE PREMISES

III. NUMBER OF SIMILAR RESPECTS

IV. RELEVANCE

V. DISANALOGIES

12.4 Refutation by Logical Analogy

Chapter 13: Casual Reasoning

Causal Reasoning	Inductive reasoning in which some effect is inferred from what is assumed to be its cause, or some cause is inferred from what is assumed to be its effect.
Cause	A word with a variety of meanings, including a necessary condition, a sufficient condition, a necessary and sufficient condition, and a critical factor in the production of a certain event.
Induction by Simple Enumeration	A type of inductive generalization that suggests that two or more phenomena always accompany one another in specified circumstances because they repeatedly accompany one another in these circumstances. Critically, causal laws cannot be tested by this method.
Inductive Generalization	The process of arriving at universal propositions from the particular facts of experience.
Method of Agreement	A common tool of scientific inquiry that looks for the sole circumstance invariably associated with a particular effect in multiple instances, and considers that circumstance the cause of the effect.
Method of Concomitant Variation	A pattern of inductive inference in which it is concluded that, when one phenomenon varies consistently with some other phenomenon in some manner, there is some causal relation between the two phenomena.
Method of Difference	A common tool of scientific inquiry that looks for the sole circumstance that varies between an instance in which an effect is produced and an instance in which the effect is not produced, and considers that circumstance part of the cause of the effect.
Method of Residues	A pattern of inductive inference in which, when some portions of the phenomenon under investigation are known be the effects of certain identified antecedents, we may conclude that the remaining portion of the phenomenon is the effect of the remaining antecedents.
Mill's Methods	The five patterns of inductive inference analyzed and formulated by John Stuart Mill; also known as the "canons of induction" or "methods of experimental inquiry."

Necessary and Sufficient Condition	The meaning of "cause" when inferences are made both from cause to effect and from effect to cause.
Necessary Condition	A circumstance in whose absence the event specified cannot occur.
Proximate Cause	In a chain of causes and effects, the event nearest to the effect.
Remote Cause	In a chain of causes and effects, an event distant from the effect.
Sufficient Condition	A circumstance in whose presence the event specified must occur.
The Joint Method of Agreement and Difference	The use of a combination of the method of agreement and the method of difference, to give the conclusion a higher degree of probability.

Chapter 13: Critical Reasoning

13.1 Cause and Effect

13.2 Casual Laws and Uniformity of Nature

13.3 Induction by Simple Enumeration

13.4 Methods of Casual Analysis

The Method of Agreement

The Method of Difference

The Joint Method of Agreement and Difference

The Method of Residues

The Method of Concomitant Variation

Limitations of Inductive Techniques

Chapter 14: Science and Hypothesis
Key Terms

Classification	The organization and division of large collections of things into an ordered system of groups and subgroups.
Compatibility with Previously Well-Established Hypotheses	A criterion for evaluating scientific hypotheses; the totality of hypotheses accepted at any one time should be consistent with each other.
Crucial Experiment	An experiment whose outcome is claimed to establish the falsehood of one of two competing and inconsistent scientific hypotheses.
Predictive or Explanatory Power	A criterion for evaluating scientific hypotheses; the range of facts deducible from a testable hypothesis.
Preliminary Hypothesis	A hypothesis, usually partial and tentative, adopted at the outset of a scientific inquiry to give direction to the collection of evidence.
Relevance	An attribute of a hypothesis, possessed when the facts to be explained are deducible from that hypothesis.
Scientific Explanation	A theoretical account of some fact or event, always subject to revision, that exhibits relevance, compatibility with previously established hypotheses, predictive power, and simplicity.
Scientific Method	The general pattern of scientific research, involving seven stages: identifying the problem, devising preliminary hypotheses, collecting additional facts, formulating the explanatory hypothesis, deducing further consequences, testing the consequences, and applying the theory.
Simplicity	A criterion for evaluating scientific hypotheses; the 'naturalness' of a hypothesis, which can be tricky to determine.
Testability	An attribute of a scientific hypothesis; its capacity to be confirmed or disconfirmed.
Unscientific Explanation	An explanation that differs from a scientific explanation chiefly in being presented and accepted dogmatically, and taken as true regardless of the evidence.

Chapter 14: Science and Hypothesis

14.1 The Value of Science

14.2 Explanations, Scientific and Unscientific

14.3 Evaluating Scientific Explanations

1. Compatibility with Previously Well-established Hypotheses

2. Predictive or Explanatory Power

3. Simplicity

14.4 Scientists in Action

I. ERATOSTHENES' MEASUREMENT OF THE CIRCUMFERENCE OF THE EARTH

II. GALILEO'S EXPERIMENT WITH FALLING OBJECTS

III. GALILEO'S EXPERIMENTS ROLLING BALLS DOWN AN INCLINED PLANE

IV. NEWTON'S DECOMPOSITION OF SUNLIGHT WITH A PRISM

V. CAVENDISH'S MEASUREMENT OF THE STRENGTH OF GRAVITY

VI. FOUCAULT'S PENDULUM

14.5 Seven Stages of Scientific Investigation

1. Identifying the Problem

2. Devising Preliminary Hypotheses

3. Collecting Additional Facts

4. Formulating the Explanatory Hypothesis

5. Deducing Further Consequences

6. Testing the Consequences

7. Applying the Theory

14.6 The Stages of Scientific Investigation Illustrated

I. THE PROBLEM

II. PRELIMINARY HYPOTHESES

III. COLLECTING ADDITIONAL FACTS

IV. FORMULATING THE REFINED EXPLANATORY HYPOTHESIS

V. AND VI. DEDUCING AND TESTING CONSEQUENCES

VII. APPLICATIONS

14.7 When Hypotheses Compete

14.8 Classification as Hypotheses

Chapter 15: Probability
Key Terms

A *Priori* Theory of Probability
A theory in which the probability of a simple event is a fraction between 0 and 1, determined by the number of outcomes in which the event in question occurs, divided by the total number of equipossible outcomes.

Addition Theorem for Events That Are Not Mutually Exclusive
A theorem in the calculus of probability asserting that the probability of one or another non-mutually exclusive alternative event occurring can be calculated in one of two ways: by analyzing the favorable cases into mutually exclusive events and summing the successful-event probabilities; or by determining the probability that no one of the alternative events will occur and subtracting that probability from zero.

Addition Theorem for Mutually Exclusive Events
A theorem in the calculus of probability asserting that the probability of one or another mutually exclusive alternative event occurring is the sum of the probabilities of each component event.

Alternative Occurrence
A complex event that consists of the occurrence of any one of two or more simple events; alternative occurrences may be mutually exclusive, or not.

Calculus of Probability
A branch of mathematics that can be used to compute the probabilities of complex events from the probabilities of their component events.

Expected Value
The value of a wager or investment, determined by multiplying each of the mutually exclusive possible returns from the wager by the probability of that return, and summing all those products.

Independent Events
Events so related that the occurrence or nonoccurrence of one has no effect on the occurrence or nonoccurrence of the other.

Joint Occurrence
A compound event in which two simple events both occur.

Mutually Exclusive Events
Events of such a nature that, if one occurs, the other(s) cannot occur.

Product Theorem for Independent Events

A theorem in the calculus of probability asserting that the probability of the joint occurrence of multiple independent events is equal to the product of their separate probabilities.

Product Theorem for Non-Independent Events

A theorem in the calculus of probability asserting that the probability of the joint occurrence of multiple non-independent events is equal to the probability of the first event times the probability of the second event if the first occurred, and so on.

The Relative Frequency Theory of Probability

A theory in which the probability of a simple event is a fraction between 0 and 1, determined by the number of members of some class that have a particular attribute, divided by the total number of members of that class.

Chapter 15: Probability

15.1 Alternative Conceptions of Probability

The *A Priori* Theory of Probability

The Relative Frequency Theory of Probability

15.2 The Probability Calculus

15.3 Probability of Joint Occurrences

15.4 Probability of Alternative Occurrences

15.5 Expectation Value

Supplemental Exercises

1.3 Arguments

Identify the premises and conclusion of the following.

1. Literature can be restored to its position of honor only if it gives up its claim of having a superior view of truth. It can't give up that claim and maintain its traditional role in academia. It's thus clear that literature can't both be restored to its position of honor and still maintain its traditional role in academia.

2. This is an inference of valid form. If this were an inference of invalid form, then its premises could be true if its conclusion were false. Now, plainly, either its premises could be true or they not. Its conclusion is not false but true.

1.5 Validity and Truth

Construct a deductive argument with two premises and a conclusion that has the following characteristics.

1. An invalid argument with both of its premises and its conclusion all true.

2. A valid argument with both of its premises and its conclusion are false.

2.1 Paraphrasing

Paraphrase the following "real world" arguments to clarify which are premises and what is the conclusion. Also diagram them to confirm their structure.

1. ① If you don't believe that this election is the most important in our life time, then all you have to do is look at the stories about the millions of middle class families who are struggling to get ahead. ② There are record bankruptcies, record foreclosure rates, and Americans owe more than $750 billion in credit card debt. ③ And last year, because the cost of tuition has soared, 220,000 young people had to give up on their dream of a better future. ④ These men and women built America. ⑤ They worked hard. ⑥ They contribute week after week. ⑦ And in return, they're told by this Administration, "You're on your own." ⑧ My friends fundamental fairness is at stake in this election. Remarks of John Kerry to the press, 4/3/2004 (http://www.johnkerry.com/pressroom/speeches/spc_2004_0423.html)

2. ① You know, one of the great statistics of this modern era is the fact that more people are owning their own home. It seems like to me, ② an optimistic society is one that encourages ownership, ③ more people owning their own business,
    ④ people owning and managing their own health care account, ⑤ people being -- own a piece of their retirement policy that they can pass on from one generation to the next, and ① people owning their own home. ⑥ I love a society in which more and more people are able to say, welcome to my home; come to my home. (Applause.)

    ⑦ This country has added more than 1.6 million minority homeowners in the past two years. ① Today, the American homeownership rate is the highest ever, and ⑧ the highest ever for minorities. ⑨ When you own something you have a vital stake in the future of your country. (Applause.) From George W. Bush's speech to the Knights of Columbus, 8/3/2004

2.2 Recognizing Arguments

Identify the premises and conclusion then paraphrase and diagram them to show how they are structured.

1. Our efforts in Iraq are doomed because we have no way to end our involvement and save face. Were we to take complete military control of the country and its inhabitants, we'd be seen as the biggest bullies in history: The most powerful nation in the world bludgeons starving, impoverished country and its people into submission. Should we decide that the Iraqi people really don't want us there, accept that judgment and leave, we'd be seen as the most irresponsible people in history: The most powerful nation in the world destroys minor country's economy, society and infrastructure and then walks away. And, if we stay on indefinitely with an ineffective local government, we'll be seen as the most incompetent imperialists in history: The most powerful nation in the world fails to rebuild or relieve victim land. It seems pretty obvious that we have to stay in charge, walk away or support a puppet regime, all of which entail a loss of face, so there we are.

2. Marx and Engels did not understand the essential workings of a modern industrialized society. Their claim was that it contained no means of allowing the workers to benefit from the growth of industry. They could not conceive of the growth of broad-based stock companies, profit-sharing programs, and, most of all, the development of the labor union.

2.3 Arguments and Explanations

Justify your identification of whether each of these problems is primarily intended to be an argument or an explanation. Indicate what the premises and conclusion are if the passage is an argument or what is being explained and what the explanation is otherwise.

1. Because his DNA is significantly different than that of *homo sapiens* and because there is as much as a 50,000-year overlap in the existence of *homo neanderthalis* and that of *homo sapiens*, it is unlikely that Neanderthal is a direct ancestor of modern humans.

2. People continually demand more and more services from the government. Facts show that there are only two workable means by which a government can raise funds – business enterprise and taxation. People do not want the government to compete with private enterprise in business fields. This makes it clear that the only option to be had, if the added services are to be provided, is increased taxation.

2.4 Complex Argumentative Passages

Analyze these passages understand their complexity.

1. I found my psychology course pretty simple, while my ethics course was challenging. My epistemology course was demanding. My logic was quite difficult though my anthropology course was not. My aesthetics course was very demanding. However my sociology course seemed fairly simple. Therefore I am likely to find all philosophy courses to be challenging while I'm probably going to find social science classes pretty uncomplicated.

2. The members of the Institute have studied more than three thousand students over a period of ten years. Many students, of course, cannot afford the Institute's services. Without exception it has been the case that the use of the Institute prepared materials has improved the students' performance on standardized tests by more than a standard deviation. Institute studies have also shown that those who do not (or cannot) avail themselves of our services are unlikely to significantly improve their standardized test scores. Your score on the LSAT was less than a standard deviation short of the score you must have to be admitted to law school. Therefore the Institute-prepared materials will guarantee that you will get the score you need. However, if you cannot afford to participate in our program, it is doubtful that you will make it into law school.

2.5 Exercises in Reasoning

Solve the following problems, showing and justifying each inference.

1. Adams, Bates, Corey, and Dawes shared friendship from childhood, but they separated for college. One went to school at Avignon (France), one to Bucknell, one to Chicago, and one to Dartmouth. Their career fields were art, botany, chemistry, and drama. What were the school and field of each of the friends?

    A. None of the held a job whose initial matched their name.

    B. Similarly, there was no match between school and name initial or school and job initial.

    C. Bates and the scientists visited their friend who was going to school in France after their junior years.

    D. Bates and Dawes never happened to have been in the state of Illinois

2. Four friends were attending the thirtieth reunion at their high school. As people are inclined to do, they were telling stories about both their memories of high school and their life since graduation. Each of them told three lies and made one true statement. Did Bud really win the lottery twice last year?

Budd – I made all-conference in three sports.
     Judd and I are business partners.
     I married a Miss America runner-up.
     I won the lottery twice last year.
Dudd – I went to Harvard on a full-ride scholarship.
     My wife won a Pulitzer Prize for her poetry.
     I was a hostage in Lebanon for six years.
     Bud only wished he could marry a Miss America runner-up.

Judd – Even though he's a sleaze, Budd and I became business partners.
    Dudd went to Harvard on a full-ride scholarship.
    I'm on the President's Council of Economic Advisors.
    Mudd has been on welfare all his adult life.
Mudd – Judd lied when he said I had been on welfare all my adult life.
    Dudd's wife did win the Pulitzer for her poetry.
    I've never accepted any form of public assistance.
    Bud's last two statements are true.

3.3 Language Forms and Language Functions

What language functions do these passages illustrate? Why?

1. The draft ruins young men by turning them into robots and brutalizing them into killing. The all-volunteer army would destroy us by establishing a state-sanctioned body of professional killers in our midst.

   It's clear that this passage is heavily loaded with emotion (expressive function), but its probable primary function is directive as it tries to persuade the reader that the draft is something that should not be implemented.

2. .In a nation-wide survey of police departments, it was recently disclosed that searches of the homes of all men arrested for sexual assault within the last three years showed the presence of one or more of the so-called "men's magazines."

   Although there is probably an underlying intent to direct us to do something to eradicate men's magazines, what we can know for sure is that we are being informed that those who commit sexual assault seem to read such publications.

3.4 Emotive and Neutral Language

*Rewrite the following in emotionally neutral language
without altering the factual content significantly.*

1. At least the Beatles were clean-cut boys in suits when they came on the scene, but today's pop stars look like they slithered out from under rocks.... These sleazy punk rock singers look like mangled victims of a car wreck. What's worse is that these weirdoes have become the idols of our youth. Is it any wonder that we've got kids with drug problems who laugh at the idea of hard work and learning?

2. We surely had to annihilate the Beast of Baghdad lest he betray our treaties and again crush his people under his malevolent heel. His treasonous rule is a blot on the face of civilized humanity. If we tolerate his brutalization of innocent women and children, we are guilty of sanctioning consummate evil.

3.5 Agreement and Disagreement in Attitude and Belief

Identify the kinds of agreement and disagreement shown by each pair.

1. a. John's devotion to his job is evidence of an obsessive attachment to work.
   b. John's dedication to his work is a sign of great responsibility.

2.   a. The Rev. Sammy Black is a despicable fraud, preying on the faithful.

       b. The Rev. Sammy Black is a dangerous fanatic, leading others to his extremism.

4.1 Disputes and Definitions

Indicate whether and why each of the following is an obviously genuine a merely verbal or an apparently verbal but really genuine dispute.

1.   **A** holds that our military incursion into Iraq was justified by Iraqi involvement in the 9/11 attacks on the United States. **B** argues that our actions were not justified because there was not then, nor has there been discovered since, any reliable evidence of any direct Iraqi participation in the planning of, supplying materials for, or execution of those attacks.

2.   **A** contends that there should be a Constitutional amendment restricting marriage to "the historical principle" of the union of one adult man and one adult woman. **B** holds that marriage should be open to any two consenting adults.

3.   **A** holds that her boss is a petty tyrant while **B**, who works for the same woman in much the same job as **A**, believes their boss is a strong and decisive leader.

4.2 Definitions and Their Uses

Explain which of the five types of definition is shown in each of the following and why it is that sort of definition.

1.   Patriotism is supporting your government no matter whether or not you agree with its decisions and actions.

2.   In order for this course to be satisfactorily completed, not only does the student have to take all the examinations and earn a composite grade of more than 60% of the possible points but also the student has to submit a term paper that demonstrates significant effort in discussing one of the topics in the syllabus.

3.   In this context we will use the term "student" to apply to anyone, graduate or undergraduate, enrolled in the course, whether for credit or not.

4.   *Homo neanderthalis* is a member of the human family but not a direct ancestor of *homo sapiens sapiens*.

5.   "Livid" means both pale and darkly discolored.

4.3 Extension, Intension and the Structure of Definitions.

Put the elements of the following in order of increasing intension.

1.   Ford Escape, motor vehicle, mode of transportation, SUV, manufactured item.

2.   dog, dachshund, chordate, animal, hound, mammal

4.4 Extension and Denotative Definition

Give three examples of each of these terms as a means of definition.

1. Author
2. Knights of the Round Table

4.5 Intension and Intensional Definition

Give a synonymous definition for each of the following.

1. Beggar
2. Potshard
3. Viking
4. Pragmatist

4.6 Rules for Definition by Genus and Difference

Criticize the following in terms of the rules for definition by genus and difference. Indicate which rule(s) are violated. If the definition is too narrow or too wide, explain why.

1. Genius is the ability to reason correctly from inadequate information.
2. A theory is something nobody believes, except the person who made it.

5.3 Fallacies of Relevance

Identify and explain the fallacies of relevance in the following.

1. There has been much questioning of the so-called Meese Report on pornography. But look at who is attacking it – Hugh Hefner and Bob Guccione – the kingpins of Playboy and Penthouse. Their own profit-seeking would force them to oppose the report, no matter what evidence it contained.

2. It has just come to my attention that you have been talking to other employees of the University about policies which you think are unfair. We know that one of them wrote the letter to the local paper cataloging misuse of public funds in his department. If you think this is such an awful place to work, I'll be glad to accept your resignation!

5.4 Fallacies of Defective Induction

Identify and explain the fallacies of defective induction in the following.

1. If you look at the First Ladies from Bess Truman and Mamie Eisenhower through Roslyn Carter, Nancy Reagan and Laura Bush, you will see that they were all attractive, soft-spoken women who avoided the lime-light as much as possible. It is surely the case, then, that if you want to become President, you must first find yourself an attractive, soft-spoken woman who avoids the lime-light as much as possible.

2. The introductory geology that is being proposed at UMR must be rejected. Two local ministers, three professors from Texas, and an exploration geologist from Utah have all said that its contents are unacceptable.

5.5 Fallacies of Presumption

Identify and explain the fallacies of presumption in the following.

1. There is no question that ghetto dwellers are of inferior stock. They live in unbelievable conditions. They let their children go to miserable schools. The crime rate in their neighborhoods is fantastic. And, of course, anyone who would allow himself or his family to live under such conditions must either not care or not understand. In either case, he must be sub-normal.

2. Recent research by our physiology department has shown that, on average, three hours of strenuous exercise (running, weigh-lifting, handball, etc.) per week lower people's blood pressure, control their blood sugar, reduce their weight and generally substantially improve their general health. Dr. Senius recently had a heart attack followed by quadruple by-pass surgery. Since he is clearly in ill-health, he needs to undertake a vigorous exercise program immediately.

5.6 Fallacies of Ambiguity

Identify and explain the fallacies of ambiguity in the following.

1. The newspaper said that the Senator's wife smashed a champagne bottle on the bow of the ship. But that's ridiculous. How could a knot of ribbon be hard enough to break a heavy glass bottle?

2. Palo Alto, California is one of the wealthiest municipalities in the nation. One estimate suggests that there is an average *per capita* income there of nearly $23,000. That's almost $100,000 for a family of four! Now this Roe character submits an application for food stamps. And where does he live? Palo Alto! It is unconscionable that his application even be read, much less accepted.

6.3 The Four Kinds of Categorical Propositions

Identify which of the forms A, E, I, or O each of the following is.

1. No holders of the title of Distinguished Teaching Professor are eligible for an Outstanding Teacher Award.

2. Many of those who played a sport are disinterested in being a fan of their sport.

3. Everyone who had contact with the victim will be considered a possible carrier of the infection.

4. Few tall, dark and handsome men are not self-centered.

6.4 Quality, Quantity, and Distribution

Identify the quantity and quality of each of the following, then indicate whether each of its terms is distributed or undistributed.

1. Few dinosaurs were the size of Tyrannosaurs or Brachiosaurs.

2. Sadly, many who are elected are not qualified to serve.

3. All computers will, in a reasonably short period of time, become obsolete.

4. No high school athlete is physically ready to play professional sports.

6.5 The Traditional Square of Opposition

Answer the following.

1. What is the contradictory of "Some quiz show contestants are smarter than they appear?"

2. What is a subcontrary of "Many scientists are also theists?"

3. If it is true that "Some songs by The Electric Onion are on VH1's list of all-time most popular recordings," can it also be true that "Some songs by The Electric Onion are on VH1's list of all-time worst recordings?"

4. Assuming the first statement (**A**.) in the following is true, what do we know about the truth or falsity of each of the others?

6.6 Further Immediate Inferences

For each of the following provide the converse, obverse and contrapositive of each statement. If any of these transformations would not follow validly indicate so.

1. Some people who claim to be religious cheat on their taxes.

2. No agent of the law should follow his personal agenda.

3. All world-class handball players are ambidextrous.

4. Some people who attempted to climb Mt. Everest didn't survive their adventure.

6.7 Existential Import and the Interpretation of Categorical Propositions

In each of the following the existential fallacy has been committed; explain the point at which the mistaken existential assumption is made.

1.
   (1) No mythological beasts have been bred in captivity. *Thus,*
   (2) Nothing bred in captivity is a mythological beast. *Thus,*
   (3) Everything born in captivity is a non-mythological beast. *Thus,*
   (4) Some non-mythological beasts have been bred in captivity.

2.
   (1) It's true that: No Martians are enrolled at Harvard. *Thus,*
   (2) It's false that: All Martians are enrolled at Harvard. *Thus,*
   (3) It's true that: Some Martians are not enrolled at Harvard.

6.8 Symbolism and Diagrams for Categorical Propositions

For each of the following, identify its form (A, E, I, or O), indicate the correct Boolean symbolism, the represent it on a Venn Diagram.

1. No student taking AP courses graduated with a straight-A average.

2. Some people of sub-Saharan African descent are blonds.

3. All members of the band devote many hours to practice.

4. Some who tried out for *American Idol* were not talented performers.

7.1 Standard-Form Categorical Syllogisms

Identify the major, minor and middle terms,
the figure and mood of the following syllogisms.

1. Many actors want to be directors.
   <u>Most producers want to be actors.</u>
   Thus some producers want to be directors.

2. No heroes are terrorists.
   <u>Some revolutionaries are terrorists.</u>
   Thus some revolutionaries are not heroic.

   Rewrite the following in standard form then indicate the mood and figure.

3. Many new paleontological discoveries are pushing back the dating of human origins because the discoveries show human characteristics in creatures that lived millions of years earlier. Human characteristics in early creatures push back the dating of human origins.

4. All private schools are considered to be educational institutions; hence all cases of private schooling are to be considered to be educational institutions, as all cases of private schooling are private schools.

7.2 The Formal Nature of Syllogistic Argument

Refute the following invalid arguments by constructing logical analogies.

1. Some rock singers are political activists.
   <u>Many political activists are ignorant of science.</u>
   Therefore most of those who are ignorant of science are rock singers.

2. All team sport athletes are cooperative.
   <u>All sports broadcasters are cooperative.</u>
   Thus all sports broadcasters are team sport athletes.

3. All robots are capable of self-directed behavior.
   <u>All robots are intelligent.</u>
   It follows that all intelligent beings are capable of self-directed behavior.

4. No one devoted to his field would deliberately falsify evidence.
   <u>All those who are devoted to their fields are scholars.</u>
   Thus no scholars would deliberately falsify evidence.

7.3 Venn Diagram Technique for Testing Syllogisms

*Write out the following syllogistic forms using **S** to represent the subject term, **M** to represent the middle term and **P** to represent the predicate term. Then check the validity of the form using Venn diagrams.*

1. **AAA-2**

2. **EIO-4**

3. **OAO-1**

4. **AII-3**

7.4 Syllogistic Rules and Syllogistic Fallacies

Name the rule(s) broken and the fallacy committed.

1. **III-2**

2. **EEA-3**

3. No one with a practical grasp of reality is a scholar.
   <u>No scholars become millionaires.</u>
   Thus all millionaires have a practical grasp of reality.

4. No member of the religious right is a leftwing radical.
   Some who support an ultra-conservative political agenda are members of the
       <u>religious right.</u>
   Thus some who support an ultra-conservative political agenda are leftwing radicals.

8.2 Reducing the Number of Terms to Three

Translate into standard form by eliminating synonyms and complements then identify the form and check its validity.

1. All legitimate actions are desirable.
   <u>All deceptions are illegitimate.</u>
   Thus no deceptions are desirable actions.

2. Some student papers are not uninteresting.
   <u>All student papers are original.</u>
   Therefore some interesting things are original.

3. Since some nutrients are hard to swallow, diet drinks are not hard to swallow, because the contents of diet drinks are non-nutrients.

4. Students who are disciplined are likely to succeed, since undisciplined students don't learn efficiently in classes and anyone who doesn't learn efficiently in classes is not likely to succeed.

8.3 Translating Categorical Propositions into Standard Form

Translate the following into standard-form categorical propositions.

1. Bats are not birds.
2. Professional soccer players are fit.
3. Senator John McCain marches to the beat of his own drum.
4. Students sometimes respect teachers.
5. Not all lawyers practice for the money.
6. Only those who are willing to study hard can understand a foreign (to them) culture.
7. All potential jurors except those who said they believed in the death penalty were excused from the jury pool.

8.4 Uniform Translation

Translate into standard form. With arguments determine their validity.

1. She participates when she wishes to.
2. Errors are tolerated only when they are made by the people in charge.
3. Although it seems difficult, logic is quite straightforward because that which seems difficult is usually quite straightforward
4. There are old pilots but there are no old-bold pilots, so it is clear that some oldsters aren't old and bold.

8.5 Enthymemes

Supply the probably missing proposition, put the argument into standard syllogistic form and then determine whether it's validity.

1. Don is despicable because he cheats.
2. When foreign trade improves the economy improves and when the economy improves things are good for everyone.
3. All members of ΓΟΟΔ fraternity have elevated social consciences. Thus Bob's sense of right and wrong in society is advanced.
4. Scientists study what interests them for only a fool ignores what interests him.

8.6 Sorites

Restructure these sorites into chains of syllogisms.

1. No rational being enjoys the pain of others.
   Those who enjoy the pain of others are in need of counseling.
   <u>Many who are in need of counseling are denied it.</u>
   Thus some of those who are denied counseling are not rational.

2. Successful football players are violent.
   Pacifists are never violent.
   Brother Francisco is a pacifist.
   Thus he doesn't play football successfully.

8.7 Disjunctive and Hypothetical Syllogisms

Identify the kind of syllogism offered and discuss its likely validity or invalidity.

1. Telemarketers are either desperate or duplicitous. This telemarketer is as honest as the day is long. She must, therefore, be desperate.

2. If God were all-powerful then He could make a stone so heavy He couldn't lift it. But if God could make a stone so heavy He couldn't lift it, then He wouldn't be all-powerful. Therefore if God were all-powerful He wouldn't be all-powerful.

3. If the erosion on the Sphinx and its enclosure were made by water then the figure must have been carved more than 12,500 years ago. Accepted Egyptology says it was carved by Khafre in about 2550 B.C.E. Thus the erosion must not be due to water.

8.8 The Dilemma

Discuss the reasonability of these dilemmas,
offering counter dilemmas when appropriate.

1. If things go well under the administration of the chair, then there seems no reason to have a chair; but if things do not go well under the administration of the chair, then there seems no reason to have a chair. Things must either go well or not. Thus there seems no reason to have a chair.

2. If we win the conflict in Iraq then we will lose face [1st-rate industrial power defeats 3rd-rate underdeveloped power]; but if we don't win it then we will lose face [3rd-rate underdeveloped power overcomes 1st-rate industrial power]. We have to win or not, so we're doomed to lose face over Iraq.

3. In selecting a mate you either wind up with someone who makes you happy or someone who makes you sad. If your mate makes you happy then you have chosen successfully. If your mate makes you sad then you have learned a lesson which will allow you to choose more wisely later, so, in an odd sense, you have chosen successfully here, too. Thus any choice of a mate is in some way successful.

9.2 The Symbols for Conjunction, Negation and Disjunction

Using the appropriate truth table definitions for the dot, wedge
and curl, determine whether the statements are true or not.

1. George Washington was our first president • ~ Abraham Lincoln was our second.

2. ~Tijuana is the capital of Mexico ᴠ Jerusalem is the capital of Egypt.

3. If Tijuana is not the capital of Mexico, then Stockholm is not the capital of Iraq.

9.3 Conditional Statements and Material Implication

Assuming that A and B are true, X and Y are false, and the values of P and Q are not known, what can be determined about the following?

1. (P v Q) ⊃ [A · ~ (X · ~ Y)]
2. [P ⊃ (Q v X)] ⊃ [(P ⊃ Q) ⊃ (P ⊃ X)]

9.4 Some Common Argument Forms

Use truth tables to determine the validity or invalidity of the following arguments.

1. p ⊃ (q · r)
   p ⊃ ~ (q v r)
   ∴ ~ p

2. q

3. p ⊃ (q v r)
   (q · r) ⊃ s
   ∴ p ⊃ s

9.8 Statement Forms and Material Equivalence

Use truth tables to determine whether these are tautologies, self-contradictions or contingent.

1. [P · (~ P v Q)] ⊃ Q
2. (~ P ⊃ ~ Q) v ~ (P ⊃ Q)
3. [P v (Q · R)] ≡ [(~ P ⊃ R) · ~ (~ P v ~ R)]

10.1 Formal Proof of Validity

Construct a formal proof of validity using the Rules of Inference. Be sure to indicate from which step(s) and by what rule you arrived at each step or your proof.

1. (P v Q) ⊃ (S · R)
   P · ~ T
   ∴ S

2. (P ⊃ Q) v (~ P ⊃ R)
   P · ~ Q
   ~ Q · S
   ∴ R

10.2 The Rule of Replacement

Construct a formal proof of validity using both the Rules of Inference and those of Replacement. Be sure to indicate from which step(s) and by what rule you arrived at each step or your proof.

1. (P ⊃ Q) v (~ P ⊃ R)
   P · ~ Q
   ∴ R

2. ~ (P · Q) · (P ⊃ R)
   ~ (~ P v ~ S)
   R · S

10.3 Proof of Invalidity

Prove the following invalid by the method os assigning values.

1. P ⊃ (Q ∨ R)
    (Q · R) ⊃ S
    ∴ P ⊃ S

2. P ≡ ~ Q
    Q ≡ ~ R
    R ≡ P
    ―――――
    R

10.4 Inconsistency

*Either construct a formal proof of validity or prove the
argument invalid through the method of assigning values.*

1.   p ≡ (q · r) , (q ∨ s) ⊃ t ⊢ ~ t ⊃ ~ p

2.   p ⊃ q , r ∨ ~ s , ~ (~ p · ~ r) ⊢ (p · q) ∨ (r · s)

10.5 Indirect Proof of Validity.

Construct in indirect proof of validity.

1.   (p ∨ ~ p) ⊃ (q · r) , (q ⊃ r) ⊢ r

10.6 Shorter Truth-Table Technique.

Show the following to be valid or invalid by the shorter truth-table method.

1.   ~ (p · q) ⊃ ~ (r ∨ s) ⊢ r ∨ q

2.   p ⊃ ~ (q ∨ r) , ~ (q · r) ⊃ s ⊢ p ⊃ s

11.4 Traditional Subject-Predicate Propositions

*Translate each of the following into quantificational symbolism using
the abbreviations suggested. Be sure not to begin with a "curl."*

1.   Both anarchists and democrats have high opinions of man. (Ax = x is an
      anarchist; Dx = x is a democrat; Hx = x has a high opinion of man.)

2.   To be permitted to play handball you have to be assigned locker space or not use
      the locker room. (Px = x is permitted to play handball; Ax = x is assigned locker
      space; Ux = x can use the locker room.)

11.5 Proving Validity

Construct a formal proof of validity for the following.

1. (x) (F x ⊃ G x)
    (∃ x) (H x · ~ G x)
    ∴ (∃ x) (H x · ~ F x)

2. (x) (A x ⊃ B x)
    (x) (~ C x ⊃ ~ B x)
    (x) (A x ⊃ C x)

11.6 Proving Invalidity

Prove the invalidity of the following arguments.

1. $(x) (C x \supset A x)$
    $\underline{(x) (D x \supset A x)}$
    $\therefore (x) (D x \supset C x)$

2. $(\exists x) (I x \cdot T x)$
    $\underline{(\exists x) (T x \cdot A x)}$
    $\therefore (\exists x) (I x \cdot A x)$

11.7 Asyllogistic Inference

Translate the following into quantificational notation using the suggested symbols.

1. Only players who were not club members were charged admission. (Px, Mx, Cx)

2. Not all students who work hard get both good grades and a good job. (Sx, Wx, Gx, Jx)

12.2 Argument by Analogy

Determine whether the following analogies are arguments or not.

1. To be seventy years old is like climbing the Alps. You reach a snow-crowned summit, and see behind you the deep valley stretching miles and miles away, and before you other summits higher and whiter, which you may have strength to climb, or may not. Then you sit down and meditate and wonder which it will be. **Henry Wadsworth Longfellow** (1807–82), U.S. poet. Letter, 13 March 1877.

2. The role of religion in society has been to develop decency, honesty character and education for the betterment of humanity. Darrow said: "[Trade unions] have done more for decency, for honesty, for education, for the betterment of the race, for the developing of character in man, than any other association of men." From this we can infer that Darrow thought of trade unionism as a religion. [**Clarence Darrow** (1857–1938), U.S. lawyer, writer. *The Railroad Trainman* (Nov. 1909).]

12.3 Appraising Analogical Arguments

1. Determine what the analogy is and what it is arguing, then determine whether each of the added pieces of information (taken separately) makes the argument stronger or weaker, or makes no impact on it
    Ruth and Keith have spent their summer vacation over the past decade traveling, visiting places they've never been before. They have always enjoyed their trips. They have decided to travel this year, too, and anticipate enjoying the trip.
    a.   Suppose that their annual travels had gone on for 20 years rather than 10.
    b.   Suppose that their travels had included the U.S., Europe, Asia and Africa.
    c.   Suppose they count their travels as among the highlights of their marriage.
    d.   Suppose that they had a baby six months ago and plan to take her along.
    e.   Suppose that Ruth has just completed her fourth one-woman art exhibit.
    f.   Suppose that they have always traveled in the spring and plan to do so again.

2. Analyze the following argument in terms of the six criteria given, then argue whether it is a good argument or not.

Harry just purchased a new Ford pickup. It's Harry's third one. Among members of Harry's family they've owned 36 such Fords over the past 50 years. None of them has ever had a lemon. Harry plans to use his new vehicle in construction, just as Harry's family has always done. He needed this one because he drove the last one up the Al-Can Highway to Alaska, used it on the job for two years, and then sold it for more than he'd originally paid for it. Harry bought his first one as a ten-year-old used truck with 140,000 miles on it. It lasted another ten years in Texas heat. He figures this one was a pretty smart purchase.

12.4 Refutation by Logical Analogy

Identify the argument being refuted and explain whether the refuting analogy succeeds or not.

Recent hypotheses have been advanced that the hatred we so much abhor in human behavior may be the result of genetic coding. The underlying data suggests that primitive humans were more likely to survive in groups than alone. Moreover, the argument runs, since different social groups (families, clans, tribes, etc.) were often in competition with each other for limited resources, developing antipathy toward other bands was a valuable survival characteristic. In time the thesis leads us to the position this developed into a genetic predisposition to hate anyone not in our "group." This makes as much sense as arguing that we all have a genetic predisposition to cannibalism. After all, there have been periods when limited availability of food made other people the easiest "crop." Looking at cases like the Donner Party or Alferd Packer show that cannibalism is a route to survival. So should we look on our neighbors as likely to eat us if they haven't made it to the store recently?

13.4 Methods of Causal Analysis

A.   The Method of Agreement

*Analyze the following inference, explaining how it is a case of the **Method of Agreement**. Discuss the limitations of this method in this attempt to determine causality.*

A young man entered college and was away from parental supervision for the first time in his life. In order to appear more sophisticated than he was, he went out drinking every weekend. On the first Saturday evening he went to Barney's and drank rum and cola. The next morning he had a terrible hangover. On the second Saturday he went to *The Golden Apple* and drank bourbon and cola. He awoke the following morning with a terrible hangover. On the third Saturday he went to a private party and drank vodka and cola. Subsequently he spent Sunday morning terribly hung-over. In the attempt to uncover the cause of his hangovers he looked at what had happened the night before the hangovers. It became clear that cola drinks cause them.

B. The Method of Difference

*Analyze the following inference, explaining how it is a case of the **Method of Difference**. Discuss the limitations of this method in this attempt to determine causality.*

Steven and Stuart are identical twins. They graduated from Central High as co-valedictorians. They both decided to major in economics at State U. The Econ Department had a very rigid curriculum, virtually specifying what courses you would take and when you would take them, so they shared almost all their classes. However, Steven decided to join a fraternity while Stuart chose to live in the residence halls. Steven graduated in the top 10% of their class, received no appealing job offers, but was given a fellowship to a prestigious graduate school. Stuart graduated about the middle of their class, was not given an deal for grad school but was given a job with a high-status consulting firm. It's clear that the choice of living arrangements made the difference in their lives.

C. The Joint Method of Agreement and Difference

*Analyze the following inference, explaining how it is a case of the **Joint Method of Agreement and Difference**. Discuss the limitations of this method in this attempt to determine causality.*

A popular ad on '50s television featured school children running into their homes shouting: "Look, Ma, no cavities!" The ads would go on to explain that, for example, two classes of the same grade within the same elementary school had been selected to test "…the effectiveness of Fluoristan (stannous fluoride) in a program of properly-applied oral hygiene and professional dental care." One of the classes was given toothpaste with the Fluoristan, the other the same toothpaste without it. At the end of a testing period, usually six months to a year, the children would be checked to determine how many dental caries they had developed. At least according to the ads, the children exposed to Fluoristan averaged two or three fewer caries than the ones not so treated. The conclusion the toothpaste company hoped was evident to the viewer was that the Fluoristan was the key to preventing cavities.

D. The Method of Residues

*Analyze the following inference, explaining how it is a case of the **Method of Residues**. Discuss the limitations of this method in this attempt to determine causality.*

Archimedes was given the assignment of determining whether the goldsmith who had constructed the king's crown had substituted base metals inside the crown for the gold he'd been given with which to make it. The king's stipulation, however, was that it was not to be damaged. The solution, according to legend, was that while getting into his bathtub he watched the water rise and intuited what would be known as Archimedes' Law. He filled a spouted pitcher to the brim with water, immersed the crown slowly, and caught the overflow. He then measured the volume of water forced out and repeated the experiment with the same volume of gold known to be pure. When he weighed the crown and the same-volume gold he saw that the crown was substantially lightened. From this he inferred that the crown had been adulterated, that the difference in weight resulted from some volume of the gold having been replaced by a lighter, less valuable metal.

E. The Method of Concomitant Variation

*Analyze the following inference, explaining how it is a
case of the **Method of Concomitant Variation**. Discuss the
limitations of this method in this attempt to determine causality.*

In the early 20ᵗʰ century women's hemlines were at the ankle and the economy
was in a recession. By the late 20's flapper hemlines were above the knee and the
stock market boomed. By the 30's hemlines had dropped to lower calf and we
were in The Great Depression. Following WW II, hemlines again rose above the
knee and the economy surged. In the 50's poodle skirts at mid-calf were the rage
and the Eisenhower administration said we were in a "rolling recession." The
60's saw the popularity of the Mini and the Micro-Mini and the Dow Jones
Industrials breaking 1000 for the first time in history. The Midi and Maxi
appeared in the 70's and the economy tanked. Since then there has been a wide
variety of "accepted" hemlines – from very brief to ankle-length – and the
economy has bounced all over. It's clear that, if women had any sense of
patriotism, they'd all go out and shorten their skirts!

14.5 Seven Stages of Scientific Discovery

Analyze the following in terms of the seven steps from this section.

One of the most puzzling phenomena in the history of humanity is the strange
case of "villages that went mad." Their most frequent occurrences were in the
Middle Ages, but there have been incidents as recently as 1976.

The first recorded case happened during the early fall of 1432 in the village of
Ste. Gertrude in Germany. A traveler found everyone in the village over the age
of about one year dead. There was food on the tables, partially eaten; there were
no signs of invaders; and there were evidences of pairs of people having literally
beaten, choked or stabbed each other to death. Some had clearly leapt from high
windows or walked in the nearby river to drown. All had died, whether rich or
poor. The traveler wrote: "From the banker's table with its white bread and
broiled dove to the miller's with its hard rolls and cheese to the serf's with its
black bread and onion soup, all sat empty as if the guests had merely excused
themselves for a moment."

A second case happened in the French town of Villiers in the early fall of 1487.
A priest reported coming out of his cell where he had been fasting to find all his
parishioners at each other's throats, "…screaming madly and obscenely as if
possessed by the Devil. And I knew that the Evil One had been present that day,
for the aroma of the village baker's fresh loaves had driven me out with the
intention of breaking my vow of hunger."

Dozens of other cases are reported, the last of which was the township of Stuart,
Manitoba on October 3, 1976. The local RCMP constable (Mountie) was
reporting to his superior in Winnipeg by radio, chatting about the church social he
had just attended where he had gorged on the mayor's wife's special baked
chicken and the pastor's wife's home-made French bread. Suddenly he began

screaming about the "…green snakes that are coming out of the microphone." He evidently tore the mike from the console, rushed into the street and was killed trying to beat a moving semi-trailer truck to death with the mike. The driver, when questioned by the Mounties, said that "he ran right in front of the speeding vehicle, pounding and screaming as he was drawn under the wheels. By the time I stopped, he was crushed and dozens of others were outside screaming and attacking anything that moved. I sealed myself up in the cab, called for help on my CB and watched as men, women and children madly killed each other. It was like a scene from Hell."

14.8 Classification as Hypothesis

What data are to be explained? What hypotheses are proposed to explain them? Evaluate the hypotheses in terms of the criteria that are detailed in section 14.3.

Recently there has been a major disturbance in the small Missouri town of Dixon. Children in the elementary school have been breaking out with severe rashes and terrible itching. It began with one 4th grader and quickly seemed to spread to most of the children in the school. The outbreak has not evidenced itself in any other school within a reasonable radius. School administrators have announced at least three times that they have "discovered" the answer to the disease. First they claimed it was an allergic reaction to bird droppings in the ceilings of the school. They closed the building, cleaned out the ceilings, and reopened classes. Children still itched. They said it was a new cleaner used on desks. They changed cleaners. Children still itched. They got a report from a doctor who said it was a "mass sociogenic illness," that is, they just convinced themselves they had it. Children still itched. One area mother suspected an attack by a small mite, driven from its usual hosts by spring rains. She treated her children and others with a natural insecticide, a club resin. None of those children now itch. It is thus clear that the mite is the true culprit in this case.

15. The Probability of Joint Occurrences

1. What is the probability of being dealt a flush? [5 cards, one suit]

2. If five horses are running a race and are exactly evenly matched, but there are no ties, what is the probability that you will pick the first two horses (not necessarily in order) to finish the race?

3. What is the probability of rolling all six numbers in six rolls of a die?

4. If you have a 1/10 chance of failing each of your six classes, what is the probability of your failing at least one?

15.4 Probability of Alternative Occurrences

1. What is the probability of rolling a fair die and getting a number divisible by either 2 or 3?

2. If you hold 3 of a kind and 2 odd cards in a game of draw poker, are you more likely to better your hand by discarding the 2 and drawing or by holding the 3 of a kind and one of the two and drawing only one? Why?

15.5 Expectation Value

1. Assume that you have $1000 to invest. Your broker suggests two stocks, a blue chip and an aggressive one. Based on her experience she tells you that the blue chip has an 87% chance of being worth $1150 in a month but a 13% chance of being worth only $900 then, while the aggressive one has a 57% chance of being worth $1640 in a month and a 43% chance of being worth only $600. Which, based on expectation, is the better investment?

2. Assume that you've been given a chance to play a new card game that costs differing amounts to play. You're allowed to cut a standard 52-card deck. You may pay $5 to pick a suit. If you cut that suit, you get $12. You may pay $3 to pick 2 denominations (like Q & K). If you cut that denomination, you get $14. You may pay $2 to pick a single denomination. Cutting correctly gives you $21. Or you can pay $1 to cut a specific card for a payoff of $50. Which is your best bet, based on expectation?

Solutions to Supplemental Exercises

1.3 Arguments

Identify the premises and conclusion of the following.

1.   Literature can be restored to its position of honor only if it gives up its claim of having a superior view of truth. It can't give up that claim and maintain its traditional role in academia. It's thus clear that literature can't both be restored to its position of honor and still maintain its traditional role in academia.

   The "thus" is a conclusion sign, indicating that the conclusion is "[L]iterature can't both be restored to its position of honor and still maintain its traditional role in academia." The premises are the other two sentences: "Literature can be restored to its position of honor only if it gives up its claim of having a superior view of truth" and "It can't give up that claim and maintain its traditional role in academia."

2.   This is an inference of valid form. If this were an inference of invalid form, then its premises could be true if its conclusion were false. Now, plainly, either its premises could be true or they not. Its conclusion is not false but true.

   The subjunctive form (the "were" and "could" in the second sentence and following) suggests that it is the initial premise and that what precedes it is the conclusion. It's often the case that the conclusion of an argument is placed "up front." In this case "This is an inference of valid form" *is* the conclusion and the other three sentences are the argument's premises.

1.5 Validity and Truth

Construct a deductive argument with two premises and a conclusion that has the following characteristics.

1.   An invalid argument with both of its premises and its conclusion all true.

   There are uncountably many possibilities here, but the easiest way to achieve this would be to make the three sentences wholly unrelated to each other. Consider the following:
   Either today is Monday or it isn't.
   Football (soccer) is the most popular sport in the world.
   Thus watermelon is a remarkably nutritious fruit.

   In this case the first premise will always be true (since it's an exhaustive and exclusive dichotomy), the second happens to be true in the modern world (but wouldn't have been so in 1000 B.C.), and the conclusion is true (but could be false if we did something silly in developing hybrids). Since it is logically and factually possible for the premises to be true and the conclusion false, the argument is invalid.

2.   A valid argument with both of its premises and its conclusion are false.

Again there are many possibilities, but this would work.

If there is no sun then sunlight floods the sky.
<u>If sunlight floods the sky then there's no way for us to know what's in our world.</u>
Thus if there's no sun in the sky then there's no way for us to know what's in our world.

Without a sun clearly there's no source of sunlight, so the first premise is false. If there's lots of sunlight then it should be easy to know what's in the world, so the second premise is also false. Even without a sun, things like sonar- or radar-like could help us know what's around us. This would make the conclusion false, too. Nevertheless, the argument is formally valid – its structure is if p then q; if q then r; thus if p then r.

2.1   Paraphrasing

Paraphrase the following "real world" arguments to clarify which are premises and what is the conclusion. Also diagram them to confirm their structure.

1.   ①   If you don't believe that this election is the most important in our life time, then all you have to do is look at the stories about the millions of middle class families who are struggling to get ahead. ② There are record bankruptcies, record foreclosure rates, and Americans owe more than $750 billion in credit card debt. ③   And last year, because the cost of tuition has soared, 220,000 young people had to give up on their dream of a better future. ④ These men and women built America. ⑤ They worked hard. ⑥ They contribute week after week. ⑦ And in return, they're told by this Administration, "You're on your own." ⑧ My friends fundamental fairness is at stake in this election. Remarks of John Kerry to the press, 4/3/2004
(http://www.johnkerry.com/pressroom/speeches/spc_2004_0423.html)

Characteristically, political arguments are rather complicated and can be "unpacked" in several ways. This argument is intended to be persuasive, but the ultimate conclusion is not stated – you're expected to "see its truth" from the premises stated. Sentences ② & ③ are clearly premises showing problems in our society. Sentences ④, ⑤, & ⑥ are intended to show that the people affected in ② & ③ are what was called "middle class families" in ①. Sentence ⑦ suggests that the problems of ② & ③ represent a struggle for such families. Sentence ⑧ is really a conclusion from another argument altogether. Unstated elements include ⑨ "Millions of middle class families who are struggling to get ahead," ⑩ "Administration indifference rejects fundamental fairness," and ⑪ "This election is the most important in our life time."

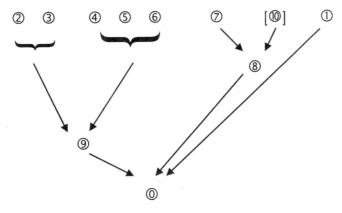

Messy, but understandable.

2. ① You know, one of the great statistics of this modern era is the fact that more people are owning their own home. It seems like to me, ② an optimistic society is one that encourages ownership, ③ more people owning their own business, ④ people owning and managing their own health care account, ⑤ people being -- own a piece of their retirement policy that they can pass on from one generation to the next, and ① people owning their own home. ⑥ I love a society in which more and more people are able to say, welcome to my home; come to my home. (Applause.)

    ⑦ This country has added more than 1.6 million minority homeowners in the past two years. ① Today, the American homeownership rate is the highest ever, and ⑧ the highest ever for minorities. ⑨ When you own something you have a vital stake in the future of your country. (Applause.) From George W. Bush's speech to the Knights of Columbus, 8/3/2004

Please notice that the same statement, for all practical purposes, occurs three times in this argument. [It's labeled ①.] And, again, as is common in political arguments, the conclusion is not stated. Here, one could reasonably suppose, that the conclusion is meant to be something like: ⑩ "An increase in the rate of homeownership suggests that we have an optimistic society in which good things are happening." An unstated intermediate conclusion is: ⓪ "We have an optimistic society."

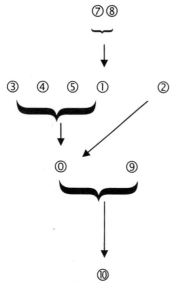

And ⑥ is an affirmation of the President's values and attitude but does not add to the content of the argument.

2.2 Recognizing Arguments

Identify the premises and conclusion then paraphrase and diagram them to show how they are structured.

1. Our efforts in Iraq are doomed because we have no way to end our involvement and save face. Were we to take complete military control of the country and its inhabitants, we'd be seen as the biggest bullies in history: The most powerful nation in the world bludgeons starving, impoverished country and its people into submission. Should we decide that the Iraqi people really don't want us there, accept that judgment and leave, we'd be seen as the most irresponsible people in history: The most powerful nation in the world destroys minor country's economy, society and infrastructure and then walks away. And, if we stay on indefinitely with an ineffective local government, we'll be seen as the most incompetent imperialists in history: The most powerful nation in the world fails to rebuild or relieve victim land. It seems pretty obvious that we have to stay in charge, walk away or support a puppet regime, all of which entail a loss of face, so there we are.

The conclusion comes up front: "Our efforts in Iraq are doomed" followed by the premise-indicator "because." The emotional statements following the colons in the next three sentences are really suggestions companion premises for each sentence's assertion. This gives us the first three premises:

① If we take military control we'll be seen as bullies.

② If we leave without resolution we'll be seen as irresponsible.

③ If we stay on with Iraqis who can't rule we'll be seen as incompetent.

116

The three companion premises:

①' If we're seen as bullies we'll lose face.
②' If we're seen as irresponsible we'll lose face.
③' If we're seen as incompetent we'll lose face.

The three intermediate conclusions generated from them:

④ If we take military control we'll lose face.
⑤ If we leave without resolution we'll lose face.
⑥ If we stay on with Iraqis who can't rule we'll lose face.

The last sentence really suggests another premise:

⑦ We have to take military control, leave without resolution or stay on.

Then there is an assumed premise:

⑧ If we lose face in Iraq, our efforts there are doomed.

All of which yields two conclusions:
⑨ We'll lose face in Iraq. *and*
⑩ Our efforts in Iraq are doomed.

The diagram makes the relationships quite clear.

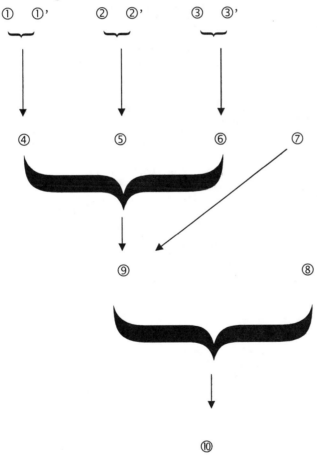

Interestingly this is a variant of an argument offered by Republican Senator George Aiken of Vermont in the waning days of the Vietnam conflict. And, although it's sound as stated, it ignores many alternative possibilities (such as our succeeding in aiding the Iraqis in their attempt to achieve responsible and effective self-government), thus leaving the conclusion open to factual dispute.

2. Marx and Engels did not understand the essential workings of a modern industrialized society. Their claim was that it contained no means of allowing the workers to benefit from the growth of industry. They could not conceive of the growth of broad-based stock companies, profit-sharing programs, and, most of all, the development of the labor union.

This argument is a good deal simpler than the previous one. The conclusion is clearly the first sentence. The second and third sentences are premises. To make the argument more acceptable, there need to

① Marx and Engels did not understand the essential workings of a modern industrialized society.

② Their claim was that it contained no means of allowing the workers to benefit from the growth of industry.

③ They could not conceive of the growth of broad-based stock companies, profit-sharing programs, and, most of all, the development of the labor union.

④ If they understood the workings of a modern industrialized society, they could conceive of stock companies, profit sharing and labor unions.

⑤ If they could conceive of stock companies, profit sharing and labor unions, they would not claim that such a society contained no means of allowing the workers to benefit from the growth of industry.

The argument then becomes a chain:

② and ⑤, therefore ③; ③ and ④, therefore ①.

The diagram is quite straightforward:

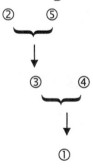

2.3 Arguments and Explanations

Justify your identification of whether each of these problems is primarily intended to be an argument or an explanation. Indicate what the premises and conclusion are if the passage is an argument or what is being explained and what the explanation is otherwise.

1. Because his DNA is significantly different than that of *homo sapiens* and because there is as much as a 50,000-year overlap in the existence of *homo neanderthalis* and that of *homo sapiens*, it is unlikely that Neanderthal is a direct ancestor of modern humans.

    The "because" (which is a premise-indicator) might lead you to believe that this is an argument, but it isn't. In this case the "because" is an explanation-indicator. The author is explaining why Neanderthal is no longer thought of as our ancestor. The explanation is pointing to current research as the clarifying material which leads us to understand why *h. neanderthalis* is now seen as he is.

2. People continually demand more and more services from the government. Facts show that there are only two workable means by which a government can raise funds – business enterprise and taxation. People do not want the government to compete with private enterprise in business fields. This makes it clear that the only option to be had, if the added services are to be provided, is increased taxation.

    This is a straightforward argument. The first three sentences are premises and the last is a conclusion.

2.4 Complex Argumentative Passages

Analyze these passages understand their complexity.

1. I found my psychology course pretty simple, while my ethics course was challenging. My epistemology course was demanding. My logic was quite difficult though my anthropology course was not. My aesthetics course was very demanding. However my sociology course seemed fairly simple. Therefore I am likely to find all philosophy courses to be challenging while I'm probably going to find social science classes pretty uncomplicated.

    In disentangling arguments it's usually most helpful to identify the multiple conclusions that are reached. In this case I am likely to find all philosophy courses to be challenging and I'll probably going to find social science classes pretty uncomplicated are the two conclusions offered even thought they occur in the same sentence. All that's needed here is to identify which premises "go with" each conclusion. The claims about courses in ethics, logic, epistemology and aesthetics support the conclusion about philosophy classes; those about psychology, anthropology and sociology buttress the inference about social science classes.

2. The members of the Institute have studied more than three thousand students over a period of ten years. Many students, of course, cannot afford the Institute's services. Without exception it has been the case that the use of the Institute prepared materials has improved the students' performance on standardized tests by more than a standard deviation. Institute studies have also shown that those who do not (or cannot) avail themselves of our services are unlikely to significantly improve their standardized test scores. Your score on the LSAT was less than a standard deviation short of the score you must have to be admitted to law school. Therefore the Institute-prepared materials will guarantee that you will get the score you need. However, if you cannot afford to participate in our program, it is doubtful that you will make it into law school.

Again two arguments are intertwined. The two conclusions, unlike the case above, are in separate sentences, but otherwise the process is the same. The first inference is that *Institute-prepared materials will guarantee that you will get the score you need* while the second conclusion is *If you cannot afford to participate in our program, it is doubtful that you will make it into law school.* Supporting both is the report that the Institute's studies have been large. The statements about how well students using Institute material do and how relatively little improvement you need for law-school admission back up the first inference. The details about the cost of the program and performance without Institute help support the second conclusion.

2.5 Exercises in Reasoning

Solve the following problems, showing and justifying each inference.

1. Adams, Bates, Corey, and Dawes shared friendship from childhood, but they separated for college. One went to school at Avignon (France), one to Bucknell, one to Chicago, and one to Dartmouth. Their career fields were art, botany, chemistry, and drama. What were the school and field of each of the friends?

   A. None of the held a job whose initial matched their name.

   B. Similarly, there was no match between school and name initial or school and job initial.

   C. Bates and the scientists visited their friend who was going to school in France after their junior years.

   D. Bates and Dawes never happened to have been in the state of Illinois

   On such problems it's usually easiest to begin by laying out a grid.

Adams	art	botany	chem	drama
Avignon				
Bucknell				
Chicago				
Dartmouth				

Bates	art	botany	chem	drama
Avignon				
Bucknell				
Chicago				
Dartmouth				

Corey	art	botany	chem	drama
Avignon				
Bucknell				
Chicago				
Dartmouth				

Dawes	art	botany	chem	drama
Avignon				
Bucknell				
Chicago				
Dartmouth				

All that is required now is to enter the information given.

Adams	art	botany	chem	drama
Avignon	A	B	B	B
Bucknell	A	B		
Chicago	A		B	
Dartmouth	A			B

Bates	art	botany	chem	drama
Avignon	C	A	C	C
Bucknell	B	A	B	B
Chicago	D	A	B	D
Dartmouth		A	C	B

Corey	art	botany	chem	drama
Avignon	B	C	A	
Bucknell		B	A	
Chicago	B	B	A	B
Dartmouth			A	B

Dawes	art	botany	chem	drama
Avignon	B	C	C	A
Bucknell		B		A
Chicago	D	D	B	A
Dartmouth	B	B	B	A

We're now in a position to draw some inferences from these grids. The only unfilled spot on Bates' grid is the intersection of "art" and "Dartmouth," so we can add

E.   Bates is the artist who went to Dartmouth.

The only open spot in the Avignon rows is under "drama" on Corey's grid, so we can add

F.   Corey is the dramatist who went to Avignon.

Adams	art	botany	chem	drama
Avignon	A	B	B	B
Bucknell	A	B		F
Chicago	A		B	F
Dartmouth	A	E	E	B

Bates	art	botany	chem	drama
Avignon	C	A	C	C
Bucknell	B	A	B	B
Chicago	D	A	B	D
Dartmouth	XXXX	A	C	B

Corey	art	botany	chem	drama
Avignon	B	C	A	XXXX
Bucknell	E	B	A	F
Chicago	B	B	A	B
Dartmouth	E	F	A	B

Dawes	art	botany	chem	drama
Avignon	B	C	C	A
Bucknell	E	B		A
Chicago	D	D	B	A
Dartmouth	B	B	B	A

The only opening on Dawes' grid is at the intersection of chemistry and Bucknell.

G.   Dawes is the chemist who went to Bucknell.

Adams	art	botany	chem	drama
Avignon	A	B	B	B
Bucknell	A	B	G	F
Chicago	A		B	F

Bates	art	botany	chem	drama
Avignon	C	A	C	C
Bucknell	B	A	B	B
Chicago	D	A	B	D

Dartmouth	A	E	E	B

Dartmouth	XXXX	A	C	B

Corey	art	botany	chem	drama
Avignon	B	C	A	XXXX
Bucknell	E	B	A	F
Chicago	B	B	A	B
Dartmouth	E	F	A	B

Dawes	art	botany	chem	drama
Avignon	B	C	C	A
Bucknell	E	B	XXXX	A
Chicago	D	D	B	A
Dartmouth	B	B	B	A

This leaves the only remaining possibility showing Adams is the botanist who went to Chicago.

2. Four friends were attending the thirtieth reunion at their high school. As people are inclined to do, they were telling stories about both their memories of high school and their life since graduation. Each of them told three lies and made one true statement. Did Bud really win the lottery twice last year?

Budd – I made all-conference in three sports.
　　　Judd and I are business partners.
　　　I married a Miss America runner-up.
　　　I won the lottery twice last year.
Dudd – I went to Harvard on a full-ride scholarship.
　　　My wife won a Pulitzer Prize for her poetry.
　　　I was a hostage in Lebanon for six years.
　　　Bud only wished he could marry a Miss America runner-up.
Judd – Even though he's a sleaze, Budd and I became business partners.
　　　Dudd went to Harvard on a full-ride scholarship.
　　　I'm on the President's Council of Economic Advisors.
　　　Mudd has been on welfare all his adult life.
Mudd – Judd lied when he said I had been on welfare all my adult life.
　　　Dudd's wife did win the Pulitzer for her poetry.
　　　I've never accepted any form of public assistance.
　　　Bud's last two statements are true.

The simplest way to work such a problem is to mark statements as true or false as you learn which they are, noting what led you to that inference. Here false statements will be boxed and true ones shaded.

Since Mudd's first & third statements are the same, they are false. That means Judd's fourth one must be true and his other three false. No one makes 2 true statements so Mudd's fourth is false & second true.

Budd　I made all-conference in three sports.
　　　Judd and I are business partners.
　　　I married a Miss America runner-up.
　　　I won the lottery twice last year.

Dudd　I went to Harvard on a full-ride scholarship.
　　　My wife won a Pulitzer Prize for her poetry.
　　　I was a hostage in Lebanon for six years.
　　　Budd only wished he could marry a Miss America runner-up.

Judd	Even though he's a sleaze, Budd and I became business partners
	Dudd went to Harvard on a full-ride scholarship.
	I'm on the President's Council of Economic Advisors.
	Mudd has been on welfare all his adult life

Mudd	Judd lied when he said I had been on welfare all my adult life.
	Dudd's wife did win the Pulitzer for her poetry.
	I've never accepted any form of public assistance.
	Budd's last two statements are true.

Judd's statement about Dudd and Harvard is false, so Dudd's must be also. Budd's statement about Judd must be false. Mudd's statement about Dudd's wife is true, so Dudd's must be too. This means that Dudd's other statements must all be false.

Budd	I made all-conference in three sports.
	Judd and I are business partners.
	I married a Miss America runner-up.
	I won the lottery twice last year.

Dudd	I went to Harvard on a full-ride scholarship.
	My wife won a Pulitzer Prize for her poetry.
	I was a hostage in Lebanon for six years.
	Budd only wished he could marry a Miss America runner-up.

Judd	Even though he's a sleaze, Budd and I became business partners
	Dudd went to Harvard on a full-ride scholarship.
	I'm on the President's Council of Economic Advisors.
	Mudd has been on welfare all his adult life

Mudd	Judd lied when he said I had been on welfare all my adult life.
	Dudd's wife did win the Pulitzer for her poetry.
	I've never accepted any form of public assistance.
	Budd's last two statements are true.

Since Dudd's statement about Budd's wife is a lie, Budd's own statement is true and all his others false.

Budd	I made all-conference in three sports.
	Judd and I are business partners.
	I married a Miss America runner-up.
	I won the lottery twice last year.

Dudd	I went to Harvard on a full-ride scholarship.
	My wife won a Pulitzer Prize for her poetry.
	I was a hostage in Lebanon for six years.
	Budd only wished he could marry a Miss America runner-up.

Judd	Even though he's a sleaze, Budd and I became business partners
	Dudd went to Harvard on a full-ride scholarship.
	I'm on the President's Council of Economic Advisors.
	Mudd has been on welfare all his adult life

Mudd	Judd lied when he said I had been on welfare all my adult life.
	Dudd's wife did win the Pulitzer for her poetry.
	I've never accepted any form of public assistance.
	Budd's last two statements are true.

This means Budd didn't win the lottery twice last year.

3.3 Language Forms and Language Functions

What language functions do these passages illustrate? Why?

1. The draft ruins young men by turning them into robots and brutalizing them into killing. The all-volunteer army would destroy us by establishing a state-sanctioned body of professional killers in our midst.

    It's clear that this passage is heavily loaded with emotion (expressive function), but its probable primary function is directive as it tries to persuade the reader that the draft is something that should not be implemented.

2. .In a nation-wide survey of police departments, it was recently disclosed that searches of the homes of all men arrested for sexual assault within the last three years showed the presence of one or more of the so-called "men's magazines."

    Although there is probably an underlying intent to direct us to do something to eradicate men's magazines, what we can know for sure is that we are being informed that those who commit sexual assault seem to read such publications.

3.4 Emotive and Neutral Language

*Rewrite the following in emotionally neutral language
without altering the factual content significantly.*

1. At least the Beatles were clean-cut boys in suits when they came on the scene, but today's pop stars look like they slithered out from under rocks.... These sleazy punk rock singers look like mangled victims of a car wreck. What's worse is that these weirdoes have become the idols of our youth. Is it any wonder that we've got kids with drug problems who laugh at the idea of hard work and learning?

    The appearance of the Beatles was within established social standards. That of today's performers in the genre is far from appropriate. Our young people look up to them. It is understandable that youth use prohibited medications and do not recognize the value of work and education.

    There are still emotional elements here, but overall it's pretty bland.

2.   We surely had to annihilate the Beast of Baghdad lest he betray our treaties and again crush his people under his malevolent heel. His treasonous rule is a blot on the face of civilized humanity. If we tolerate his brutalization of innocent women and children, we are guilty of sanctioning consummate evil.

We had to remove Saddam Hussein to keep him from continuing his going against agreements and maltreating his people. His actions are improper and if we do not counter them we bear some accountability for them.

Again there's mild emotion left, but most of it is neutralized.

3.5   Agreement and Disagreement in Attitude and Belief

Identify the kinds of agreement and disagreement shown by each pair.

1.   a. John's devotion to his job is evidence of an obsessive attachment to work.
b. John's dedication to his work is a sign of great responsibility.

Both cases agree in their belief that John spends great time and effort on his job, but they disagree in their attitudes about the suitability of such an approach to work – a. thinks it's pathological while b. thinks it's enviable.

2.   a. The Rev. Sammy Black is a despicable fraud, preying on the faithful.
b. The Rev. Sammy Black is a dangerous fanatic, leading others to his extremism.

Both agree in their negative attitude toward Rev. Black, but disagree in their belief about the sincerity of his faith.

4.1   Disputes and Definitions

Indicate whether and why each of the following is an obviously genuine a merely verbal or an apparently verbal but really genuine dispute.

1.   **A** holds that our military incursion into Iraq was justified by Iraqi involvement in the 9/11 attacks on the United States. **B** argues that our actions were not justified because there was not then, nor has there been discovered since, any reliable evidence of any direct Iraqi participation in the planning of, supplying materials for, or execution of those attacks.

This is probably an *obviously genuine dispute*, although there actually seems to be a bit of agreement here. Both seem to believe that direct Iraqi participation in planning, supplying and performing the 9/11 attacks would serve as justification for our commencement of hostilities against them. Their dispute concerns the factual question of whether we had reliable evidence of their explicit contribution to the attacks. If all the intelligence information we had at our disposal were to be de-classified, be examined and have the reason for seeing is as proof or not spelled out, we should be able to see whose belief is correct. [Of course, we may still be left with a dispute about exactly what such evidence "proves."]

125

2.   **A** contends that there should be a Constitutional amendment restricting marriage to "the historical principle" of the union of one adult man and one adult woman. **B** holds that marriage should be open to any two consenting adults.

This dispute can be spelled out in many ways. It might be easy to argue that it's merely verbal, that by "marriage" **A** probably means the sacrament of marriage as traditionally viewed by conservative Christianity, while **B** likely means a civil union that grants rights like joint tax filing, inheritance and visitation rights, etc. But, in our real world, the dispute seems to go further. In particular, it seems, most people who support a so-called "marriage amendment" are also opposed to civil union statutes and the extension of "marriage-like rights" to anyone. They do not just want their own religious denomination to refuse to perform a wedding for same-gender couples; they want to prevent any other denomination from doing so, too. They want the civil relationship joining two adults to have the same requirement of an adult, unmarried couple of opposite genders as the one their religious view demands. Given such a likely conviction, this dispute is almost certainly not only genuine but also irresolvable.

3.   **A** holds that her boss is a petty tyrant while **B**, who works for the same woman in much the same job as **A**, believes their boss is a strong and decisive leader.

This is probably a verbal dispute, although there is surely some difference in attitude exhibited. In all likelihood, were we to get **A** to clarify what behaviors she sees as characteristic of a petty tyrant (i.e., define "petty tyrant), we would get the same conduct that **B** would use to define a strong and decisive leader. There might be some genuine dispute about whether such conduct is desirable or not but, once the terms were made clear, the apparent descriptive dispute would be seen as fundamentally verbal.

4.2 Definitions and Their Uses

Explain which of the five types of definition is shown in each of the following and why it is that sort of definition.

1.   Patriotism is supporting your government no matter whether or not you agree with its decisions and actions.

This is a *persuasive definition*, designed to convince the listener (or reader) to mindlessly accept governmental activities.

2.   In order for this course to be satisfactorily completed, not only does the student have to take all the examinations and earn a composite grade of more than 60% of the possible points but also the student has to submit a term paper that demonstrates significant effort in discussing one of the topics in the syllabus.

Although not specifically described as a definition, this is a *precising definition* of "satisfactory completion" in the context of a particular course. It was probably developed to close a loophole that might have allowed the student to sidestep the term paper in an earlier statement of course requirements. For example, if there were four 100-point exams and a 100-point term paper, without this precising definition a student could do brilliantly on the exams (say, scoring 100% on each), turn in no paper and still have an 80% for the course – likely a B. Here the paper must be done, too.

3. In this context we will use the term "student" to apply to anyone, graduate or undergraduate, enrolled in the course, whether for credit or not.

    This is a *stipulative definition*. Academic administration often makes such definitions in the attempt to ensure that evaluations of teaching loads are made using the same criteria.

4. *Homo neanderthalis* is a member of the human family but not a direct ancestor of *homo sapiens sapiens*.

    This is a *theoretical definition* of our friend the Neanderthal. It reflects current scientific beliefs and evidence concerning his species and ours.

5. "Livid" means both pale and darkly discolored.

    This odd statement of two opposed meanings of the term "livid" is a pair of *lexical definitions* combined. It has the curious effect of meaning that the sentence *He was livid with rage* would be appropriate whether the person in question had had his face become a blue-black-purple (as if engorged with blood) or had had it become a pale, ashen grey (as if the blood had drained from it).

4.3 Extension, Intension and the Structure of Definitions.

Put the elements of the following in order of increasing intension.

1. Ford Escape, motor vehicle, mode of transportation, SUV, manufactured item.

    manufactured item, mode of transportation, motor vehicle, SUV, Ford Escape

    You could make a case for reversing "manufactured item" and "mode of transportation" since some manufactured items are modes of transport (like cars, trucks, trains, unicycles, etc.) while others are not (like mailboxes, swimming pools, monuments, etc.) and some modes of transportation are manufactured items (like cars, trucks, trains, unicycles, etc.) while some are not (like horses, feet, logs floating down a river, etc.). Whichever you put first, motor vehicles are more specific than either, SUVs are a sub-class of motor vehicles, and the Escape is one of dozens of SUVs.

2.   dog, dachshund, chordate, animal, hound, mammal

animal, chordate, mammal, dog, hound, dachshund

This is a pretty simple following of traditional species-genus differentiation.

4.4   Extension and Denotative Definition

Give three examples of each of these terms as a means of definition.

1.   Author

Shakespeare, Jules Verne, Ellis Peters

Although their fields differ – plays, fantasy/science fiction, medieval mysteries – all three were writers. One could, of course, have picked poets, non-fiction writers, etc. All are authors.

2.   Knights of the Round Table

Bedivere, Kay, Lancelot

(Also Gawain, Geraint, Galahad, Gareth, Gaheris, Bors, Lamorak, Percivale, Tristan, Mordred, Lionell, among others – there are 25 names inscribed on the Winchester Round Table which dates from the 13th century.)

4.5   Intension and Intensional Definition

Give a synonymous definition for each of the following.

1.   Beggar

Mendicant

2.   Potshard

A fragment of broken pottery, especially one found in an archaeological excavation

3.   Viking

Any of the Scandinavian people who raided the coasts of Europe from the 8th to the 11th centuries

4.   Pragmatist

1: an adherent of philosophical pragmatism

2: a person who takes a practical approach to problems and is concerned primarily with the success or failure of her actions

4.6 Rules for Definition by Genus and Difference

Criticize the following in terms of the rules for definition by genus and difference. Indicate which rule(s) are violated. If the definition is too narrow or too wide, explain why.

1. Genius is the ability to reason correctly from inadequate information.

    This is ambiguous because the reasoning mentioned needs to be differentiated from mere lucky guessing. It's also too narrow, seeming to exclude, for example, someone like Mozart whose genius would seem to be in his creative, not his reasoning skill. Curiously this definition also seems to be too broad, for it would seem to include the whole group of humans called *Idiot Savants*. They seem to have IQs of about 25. They are incapable of learning, writing or reading, yet they have unlimited access to specific, accurate knowledge in the fields of mathematics, music, and other precise areas. The only way to exclude them from this definition is to accompany it with a précising definition of "reason."

2. A theory is something nobody believes, except the person who made it.

    This one is funny, and might be true in some cases, but it really doesn't give us anything by which to tell whether something is a theory or not. It violates Rule 4 – ambiguous, obscure and figurative.

5.3 Fallacies of Relevance

Identify and explain the fallacies of relevance in the following.

1. There has been much questioning of the so-called Meese Report on pornography. But look at who is attacking it – Hugh Hefner and Bob Guccione – the kingpins of Playboy and Penthouse. Their own profit-seeking would force them to oppose the report, no matter what evidence it contained.

    This is an *Ad Hominem*, abusive, fallacy. Hefner and Guccione are attacked not for their arguments but for the fact that the report's acceptance might cause them financial damage. The crucial question of whether their criticisms are justified is entirely ignored.

2. It has just come to my attention that you have been talking to other employees of the University about policies which you think are unfair. We know that one of them wrote the letter to the local paper cataloging misuse of public funds in his department. If you think this is such an awful place to work, I'll be glad to accept your resignation!

    Although there is no explicit threat made here, it's pretty clear that the speaker is threatening the person's employment. There's no attempt to discuss the problems that apparently exist or to thrash out concerns of the employee. Such arguments are instances of the *Ad Baculum* fallacy. [A supervisor could explain how a public perception of misconduct, financial irregularities and employee discontent might lead to actions by the legislature or board of trustees which could impact many people's employment. If done **very** carefully, such a conversation might not be a threat (and thus this fallacy). It is possible to describe a threatening situation without doing the threatening – if I tell you a tornado is on the way, I'm warning you, not threatening you with its forces.]

5.4 Fallacies of Defective Induction

Identify and explain the fallacies of defective induction in the following.

1. If you look at the First Ladies from Bess Truman and Mamie Eisenhower through Roslyn Carter, Nancy Reagan and Laura Bush, you will see that they were all attractive, soft-spoken women who avoided the lime-light as much as possible. It is surely the case, then, that if you want to become President, you must first find yourself an attractive, soft-spoken woman who avoids the lime-light as much as possible.

   This one is a *False Cause* in particular a *post hoc ergo propter hoc*. While numerous such women have been First Ladies, there's little to suggest that having such a wife has any causal impact on your getting the job. There's also some question of relevant information being ignored. After all, what of Dolly Madison, Edith Wilson, Eleanor Roosevelt, Jackie Kennedy and Hilary Clinton? None of them was a shrinking violet yet their husbands were still elected.

2. The introductory geology that is being proposed at UMR must be rejected. Two local ministers, three professors from Texas, and an exploration geologist from Utah have all said that its contents are unacceptable.

   Here we have a question of the appropriateness of the authorities cited. We're shown no special competence in geology for the ministers, not told what the expertise of the Texas professors might be (ceramics, marketing, medicine?) and are given no clarification of what the source of the Utah geologist's opposition might be. Without much more inspection of the **reasons** they're opposed to the course, there seems little wisdom in rejecting it. At best their resistance suggests that we might want further analysis of the course's contents, preferably by recognized experts in geology.

5.5 Fallacies of Presumption

Identify and explain the fallacies of presumption in the following.

1. There is no question that ghetto dwellers are of inferior stock. They live in unbelievable conditions. They let their children go to miserable schools. The crime rate in their neighborhoods is fantastic. And, of course, anyone who would allow himself or his family to live under such conditions must either not care or not understand. In either case, he must be sub-normal.

The conclusion is that people in the ghetto are "of inferior stock." But the last two sentences (which serve as part of the premises of the argument) amount to the same thing. If you assume the conclusion you're trying to prove as part of your premises, then it's certainly the case that you can substantiate it, but your verification is trivial. You have a *circular argument* and went nowhere.

2. Recent research by our physiology department has shown that, on average, three hours of strenuous exercise (running, weigh-lifting, handball, etc.) per week lower people's blood pressure, control their blood sugar, reduce their weight and generally substantially improve their general health. Dr. Senius recently had a heart attack followed by quadruple by-pass surgery. Since he is clearly in ill-health, he needs to undertake a vigorous exercise program immediately.

The general evidence of the value of exercise might even apply to Dr. Senius if it were take under a physician's guidance and worked up gradually. We're told here that he is currently in frail health and, thus, would surely need to show great caution in undertaking an exercise program. His specific, and atypical, condition probably exempts him from the general focus on vigorous exercise. This is an *Accident* fallacy.

5.6 Fallacies of Ambiguity

Identify and explain the fallacies of ambiguity in the following.

1. The newspaper said that the Senator's wife smashed a champagne bottle on the bow of the ship. But that's ridiculous. How could a knot of ribbon be hard enough to break a heavy glass bottle?

There's a misunderstanding of the term "bow" in the first sentence. The writer has taken it to mean "A knot usually having two loops and two ends; a bowknot" while the paper surely means "The front section of a ship or boat." This confusion could only occur in print, where the two words are spelled identically. Aurally (i.e., by ear) they're pronounced differently – the ribbon "bow" is pronounced to rhyme with "go" while the ship "bow" is pronounced to rhyme with "how." It's unlikely that they'd be confused if correctly spoken. It's a fallacy of *equivocation*.

2. Palo Alto, California is one of the wealthiest municipalities in the nation. One estimate suggests that there is an average *per capita* income there of nearly $23,000. That's almost $100,000 for a family of four! Now this Roe character submits an application for food stamps. And where does he live? Palo Alto! It is unconscionable that his application even be read, much less accepted.

The problem is one of averages. Roe may well earn little enough to qualify for food stamps. One family earning $1,000,000 a year would "average out" nine others earning nothing. This is a fallacy of *division*. It's like the concern that, since ¼ of the children born in the world each year are Chinese, your Scandinavian brother and sister's expected baby (their 4th) will be Chinese. The general conditions don't necessarily apply to individual cases.

6.3   The Four Kinds of Categorical Propositions

Identify which of the forms A, E, I, or O each of the following is.

1. No holders of the title of Distinguished Teaching Professor are eligible for an Outstanding Teacher Award.

    The initial "No" is the tip-off. Generally it's a sign that you have an **E** proposition. In this case we're being told that all holders of the title of Distinguished Teaching Professor are excluded from the group of those eligible for an Outstanding Teacher Award.

2. Many of those who played a sport are disinterested in being a fan of their sport.

    From a categorical point of view, "many" is a synonym for "some." Reading this statement in a straightforward way shows us that there are some people both who played a sport are disinterested in being a fan of that sport. This makes it appear that we have an **I** proposition. It is possible, however, to read "disinterested" as "not interested." If that is a correct interpretation of the term then, given the negative predicate term, the statement might better be read as an **O** proposition. The best way to determine whether "disinterested" should be taken to stand for "not interested" is to determine whether it is the complement of "interested." [To be the complement means that the two, together, cover all possibilities. Generally be know that two complementary terms are *exhaustive* and *exclusive*, i.e., every possibility must be one or the other but cannot be both. Blue and non-blue are complementary; if something is blue it cannot be non-blue, and *vice versa*.] In the analysis of this statement the question is whether "interested" and "disinterested" complementary. The terms certainly are exclusive; the issue is whether they are exhaustive. Commonly the antonym of "interested" is "indifferent," while the synonym of "disinterested is "impartial." One might, then, be interest but impartial. It appears that "disinterested" isn't a proper complement of "interested" and the statement actually is an **I** proposition. It was, however, worthwhile considering the possibility that "disinterested" here meant "not interested."

3. Everyone who had contact with the victim will be considered a possible carrier of the infection.

    The "Every" is a dependable indicator of an **A** proposition. This statement certainly claims that all those who had contact with the victim are also included in the category of those who are possible carriers.

1.   Few tall, dark and handsome men are not self-centered.

"Few," like "many," serves the same role as "some." The "not" tells us we have a negative proposition. Put particular and negative together and you have an **O** proposition.

6.4 Quality, Quantity, and Distribution

Identify the quantity and quality of each of the following, then indicate whether each of its terms is distributed or undistributed.

1.   Few dinosaurs were the size of Tyrannosaurs or Brachiosaurs.

"Few" tells us this statement has a particular quantity; the lack of a "not" (or similar term) shows us it has an affirmative quality. Affirmative propositions have undistributed predicates; particular ones have undistributed subjects. When this information is pulled together, we can infer that this is a particular affirmative proposition (i.e., an **I**) that has no distributed terms.

2.   Sadly, many who are elected are not qualified to serve.

"Many" tells us this statement has a particular quantity; the occurrence of a "not" (or similar term) shows us it has a negative quality. Negative propositions have distributed predicates; particular ones have undistributed subjects. When this information is pulled together, we can infer that this is a particular negative proposition (i.e., an **O**) that has a distributed predicate and undistributed subject.

3.   All computers will, in a reasonably short period of time, become obsolete.

"All" indicates a universal quantity; the lack of a "not" (or similar term) shows us it has an affirmative quality. Universal propositions have distributed subjects; affirmative propositions have undistributed predicates. When this information is pulled together, we can infer that this is a universal affirmative proposition (i.e., an **A**) that has a distributed subject and an undistributed predicate.

4.   No high school athlete is physically ready to play professional sports.

As was indicated in the last set of exercises the "No" designates a universal negative (**E**) proposition: universal quantity, negative quality, distributed subject and predicate.

6.5 The Traditional Square of Opposition

Answer the following.

1.   What is the contradictory of "Some quiz show contestants are smarter than they appear?"

The contradictory of an **I** is an **E**. "No quiz show contestants are smarter than they appear."

2.   What is a subcontrary of "Many scientists are also theists?"

Only **I** and **O** propositions can be subcontraries. The subcontrary of any particular proposition can be generated by changing the quality of the proposition. In this case that yields "Many scientists are not theists."

3.   If it is true that "Some songs by The Electric Onion are on VH1's list of all-time most popular recordings," can it also be true that "Some songs by The Electric Onion are on VH1's list of all-time worst recordings?"

Of course they can both be true. It's not uncommon for music that's immensely popular when it first appears to be seen later as having been terrible. **Blender Magazine** has a fan's suggestion that Kim Carnes' recording *Betty Davis Eyes* should be counted as one of its worst 50 songs (http://www.blender.com/articles/article_786.html); **The Golden Age of Rock Music** lists it as one of the two All-Time Top 40 songs from the 80s (http://www.mazeministry.com/↵ publishedworks/magazines/elks/elksmaintext.htm).

4.   Assuming the first statement (**A**.) in the following is true, what do we know about the truth or falsity of each of the others?

A   All teachers are entertainers.

B   No teachers are entertainers.

This is the contrary of **A**, so they cannot both be true. Since we're told that **A** is true, **B** must be false.

C   Some teachers are entertainers.

This is the subaltern of **A** so, since its superaltern is assumed true, it must be true also.

D   Some teachers are not entertainers.

This is the contradictory of **A**. Since they must have opposite truth values, it must be false.

6.6 Further Immediate Inferences

For each of the following provide the converse, obverse and contrapositive of each statement. If any of these transformations would not follow validly indicate so.

1. Some people who claim to be religious cheat on their taxes.

    Converse: Some people who cheat on their taxes claim to be religious

    Obverse: Some people who claim to be religious don't fail to cheat on their taxes.

    Contrapositive: Some people who don't cheat on their taxes don't claim to be religious. *Not valid* (see **Introduction to Logic**, p. 196

2. No agent of the law should follow his personal agenda.

    Converse: No one who follows his personal agenda should be an agent of the law.

    Obverse: All agents of the law should avoid following his personal agenda.

    Contrapositive: No person who fails to follow his personal agenda should not be an agent of the law. *Not valid* (see p. 196 in **Introduction to Logic**) In the non-Boolean interpretation the contraposition by limitation would be "Some people who fail to follow their personal agendas should not not be agents of the law."

3. All world-class handball players are ambidextrous.

    Converse: All ambidextrous people are world-class handball players. *Not valid* (see p. 192 in **Introduction to Logic.**) In the non-Boolean sense it could be "Some ambidextrous people are world-class handball players." (by limitation)

    Obverse: No world-class handball players are not ambidextrous.

    Contrapositive: All non-ambidextrous people are not world-class handball players. (or, more simply, "No non-ambidextrous people are world-class handball players."

4. Some people who attempted to climb Mt. Everest didn't survive their adventure.

    Converse: Some people who didn't survive their adventure attempted to climb Mt. Everest. *Not valid* (see p. 192 in **Introduction to Logic**)

    Obverse: Some people who attempted to climb Mt. Everest were non-survivors of their adventure.

    Contrapositive: Some people who didn't fail to survive didn't attempt to climb Mt. Everest.

6.7 Existential Import and the Interpretation of Categorical Propositions

In each of the following the existential fallacy has been committed; explain the point at which the mistaken existential assumption is made.

1. (1) No mythological beasts have been bred in captivity. *Thus,*
   (2) Nothing bred in captivity is a mythological beast. *Thus,*
   (3) Everything born in captivity is a non-mythological beast. *Thus,*
   (4) Some non-mythological beasts have been bred in captivity.

   The inference from (3) to (4) is invalid – it's conversion by limitation, valid by the traditional interpretation but not in the Boolean one since it entails that there are non-mythological beasts. That happens to be true in our universe, but wouldn't have to be.

2. (1) It's true that: No Martians are enrolled at Harvard. *Thus,*
   (2) It's false that: All Martians are enrolled at Harvard. *Thus,*
   (3) It's true that: Some Martians are not enrolled at Harvard.

   The inference from (2) to (3) is invalid. It would entail that Martians *do* exist.

6.8 Symbolism and Diagrams for Categorical Propositions

For each of the following, identify its form (A, E, I, or O), indicate the correct Boolean symbolism, the represent it on a Venn Diagram.

1. No student taking AP courses graduated with a straight-A average.

   E proposition

   S = is a student taking AP courses; G = graduated with a straight-A average

   SG = 0

   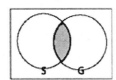

2. Some people of sub-Saharan African descent are blonds.

   I proposition

   S = is a person of sub-Saharan descent; B = is a blond

   SB ≠ 0

   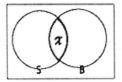

3. All members of the band devote many hours to practice.

    A proposition

    B = is a member of the band; D = devotes many hours to practice

    B $\overline{\text{D}}$ = 0

    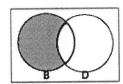

4. Some who tried out for *American Idol* were not talented performers.

    O proposition

    A = tried out for *American Idol*; T = was a talented performer

    A $\overline{\text{T}}$ ≠ 0

    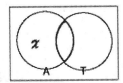

7.1 Standard-Form Categorical Syllogisms

*Identify the major, minor and middle terms,
the figure and mood of the following syllogisms.*

1. Many actors want to be directors.
    <u>Most producers want to be actors.</u>
    Thus some producers want to be directors.

    The subject term of the conclusion is the minor term: *producers*
    The predicate term of the conclusion is the major term:
    those who want to be directors
    The middle term is the one common to both premises: *actors*
    The major premise is an I; the minor premise is an **I**; the conclusion
    is an **I**; the middle term is the subject of the major and predicate of
    the minor, so the syllogism is in the first figure and is an **III-1**

2. No heroes are terrorists.
    <u>Some revolutionaries are terrorists.</u>
    Thus some revolutionaries are not heroic.

    The subject term of the conclusion is the minor term: *revolutionaries*
    The predicate term of the conclusion is the major term: *heroes*
    The middle term is the one common to both premises: *terrorists*
    The major premise is an **E**; the minor premise is an **I**; the conclusion is
    an **O**; the middle term is the predicate of both major and the minor, so the
    syllogism is in the second figure and is an **EIO-2**

Rewrite the following in standard form then indicate the mood and figure.

3. Many new paleontological discoveries are pushing back the dating of human origins because the discoveries show human characteristics in creatures that lived millions of years earlier. Human characteristics in early creatures push back the dating of human origins.

    All human characteristics in early creatures that lived millions of years earlier push back the dating of human origins.
    All new paleontological discoveries show human characteristics in early creatures.
    Thus many of these discoveries are pushing back the dating of human origins.

    > Major term: *things that push back the dating of human origins*; Minor term: *new paleontological discoveries*; Middle term: *human characteristics*... **AAI-1**

4. All private schools are considered to be educational institutions; hence all cases of private schooling are to be considered to be educational institutions, as all cases of private schooling are private schools.

    All cases of private schooling are private schools.

    All private schools are considered to be educational intuitions.

    Thus all cases of private schooling are to be considered to be educational institutions.

    > Major term: *educational institutions*; Minor term: *cases of private schooling*; Middle term: *private schools* **AAA-4**

7.2   The Formal Nature of Syllogistic Argument

Refute the following invalid arguments by constructing logical analogies.

1. Some rock singers are political activists.
    Many political activists are ignorant of science.
    Therefore most of those who are ignorant of science are rock singers.

    Some roses are fragrant.
    Many fragrant things are artificial chemical solutions.
    Therefore most artificial chemical solutions are roses.

2. All team sport athletes are cooperative.
    All sports broadcasters are cooperative.
    Thus all sports broadcasters are team sport athletes.

    All dogs are animals.
    All cats are animals.
    All cats are dogs.

138

3. All robots are capable of self-directed behavior.
   All robots are intelligent.
   It follows that all intelligent beings are capable of self-directed behavior.

   All bacteria are alive.
   All bacteria are very small.
   All very small things are alive.

4. No one devoted to his field would deliberately falsify evidence.
   All those who are devoted to their fields are scholars.
   Thus no scholars would deliberately falsify evidence.

   No cats are fish.
   All cats are vertebrates.
   Thus no vertebrates are fish.

7.3 Venn Diagram Technique for Testing Syllogisms

*Write out the following syllogistic forms using **S** to represent the subject term, **M** to represent the middle term and **P** to represent the predicate term. Then check the validity of the form using Venn diagrams.*

1. **AAA-2**

   All **P** are **M**
   All **S** are **M**
   Thus all **S** are **P**

   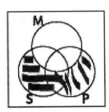

   Since there is non-empty space in **S** outside **P**, this is invalid.

2. **EIO-4**

   No **P** are **M**
   Some **M** are **S**
   Thus some **S** are not **P**

   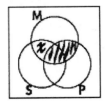

   Since there is a member inside **S** and outside **P**, this is valid.

3. **OAO-1**

Some **M** are not **P**
Some **A** are **M**
Thus some **S** are not **P**

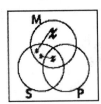

Since there is no certain member inside **S** and outside **P**, this is invalid. [There is a member that is $\overline{S}$ M $\overline{P}$ or S M $\overline{P}$ and there is one that is S M P or S M $\overline{P}$ – so a single S M $\overline{P}$ member would satisfy both cases – but it's not necessary that there be an S M $\overline{P}$ member at all – the premises could be satisfied with an $\overline{S}$ M $\overline{P}$ and an S M P.]

4. **AII-3**

All **M** are **P**
Some **M** are **S**
Thus some **S** are **P**

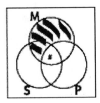

Since we see that there is a member inside an intersection of **S** and **P**, we know the syllogism is valid.

7.4 Syllogistic Rules and Syllogistic Fallacies

Name the rule(s) broken and the fallacy committed.

1. **III-2**

With all particular affirmative statements, no term is distributed. This violates Rule 2, and thus commits the Fallacy of the undistributed middle.

2. **EEA-3**

With both premises being universal negative statements this syllogism violates Rule 4, and thus commits the Fallacy of exclusive premises

3. No one with a practical grasp of reality is a scholar.
No scholars become millionaires.
Thus all millionaires have a practical grasp of reality.

This is an **EEA-4** and like # 2 above has two universal negative premises, so violates Rule 4 and commits the Fallacy of exclusive premises.

4. No member of the religious right is a leftwing radical.
    Some who support an ultra-conservative political agenda are members of the
        religious right.
    Thus some who support an ultra-conservative political agenda are leftwing
    radicals.

    This is an **EII-1**. It has an affirmative conclusion but a negative
    major premise, so violates Rule 5 and commits the fallacy of
    drawing an affirmative conclusion from a negative premise. It also
    violates Rule 3 since its major term of leftwing radical is
    distributed in the major premise but not in the conclusion. There
    it commits an illicit major fallacy.

8.2 Reducing the Number of Terms to Three

*Translate into standard form by eliminating synonyms and
complements then identify the form and check its validity.*

1. All legitimate actions are desirable.
    All deceptions are illegitimate.
    Thus no deceptions are desirable actions.

    All legitimate actions are desirable.
    No deceptions are legitimate.
    Thus no deceptions are desirable actions.

    AEE-1   Invalid – violates undistributed middle (Rule 2)

2. Some student papers are not uninteresting.
    All student papers are original.
    Therefore some interesting things are original.

    All student papers are original.
    Some student papers are interesting.
    Therefore some interesting things are original.

    AII-3 Valid

3. Since some nutrients are hard to swallow, diet drinks are not hard to swallow,
    because the contents of diet drinks are non-nutrients.

    Some nutrients are hard to swallow.
    No diet drinks are nutrients.
    Thus no diet drinks are hard to swallow things.

    IEE-1 Invalid (Rule 2 – undistributed middle)

4. Students who are disciplined are likely to succeed, since undisciplined students
    don't learn efficiently in classes and anyone who doesn't learn efficiently in
    classes is not likely to succeed.

    All students who are likely to succeed are ones who learn
    efficiently.

<u>All students who learn efficiently in class are disciplined.</u>
Thus all students who are disciplined are likely to succeed.

AAA-4   Invalid (Rule 2 – undistributed middle)

8.3   Translating Categorical Propositions into Standard Form

Translate the following into standard-form categorical propositions.

1.   Bats are not birds.

     Since this surely is meant to be a statement about all bats, its standard form is All bats are birds.

2.   Professional soccer players are fit.

     Although probably not true, this too is meant to be a universal claim All professional soccer players are people who are fit.

3.   Senator John McCain marches to the beat of his own drum.

     This singular proposition is treated as a universal proposition whose form is (All) Senator John McCain is a person who marches to the beat of his own drum

4.   Students sometimes respect teachers.

     This one is more difficult to "unpack." The "first glance" interpretation might be Some students are people who respect teachers, but this doesn't include the time element of *sometimes*. You could shift to Some points in time are times at which students respect teachers, but that might be interpreted as saying those points had all students respecting teachers then. Probably best, although it suggests multiple-layered quantification, would be Some points in time are times at which some students respect teachers. That would allow the statement to be true of all students but would not require it.

5.   Not all lawyers practice for the money.

     If you start by ignoring the "not," you'd have an obvious **A** proposition All lawyers are people who practice for money. The "not' denies that, i.e., contradicts it. The contradictory of an **A** is the related **O** (from the Square of Opposition) so this says Some lawyers are people who don't practice for money.

6. Only those who are willing to study hard can understand a foreign (to them) culture.

Following the obvious pattern of "Only women are nuns" being read as "All nuns are women," this becomes All those who come to understand a foreign (to them) culture are those who are willing to study hard.

7. All potential jurors except those who said they believed in the death penalty were excused from the jury pool.

All potential jurors who did not say they believed in the death penalty were excused from the jury pool.

8.4 Uniform Translation

Translate into standard form. With arguments determine their validity.

1. She participates when she wishes to.

All times when she wishes to participate are times when she does participate.

2. Errors are tolerated only when they are made by the people in charge.

All errors that are tolerated are errors committed by people in charge.

3. Although it seems difficult, logic is quite straightforward because that which seems difficult is usually quite straightforward

Some things that seem difficult are things that are quite straightforward.
(All) logic is a thing that seems difficult.
Thus (all) logic is a thing that is quite straightforward.

IAA-1   Invalid (Rule 6 – Existential fallacy)

4. There are old pilots but there are no old-bold pilots, so it is clear that some oldsters aren't old and bold.

No pilots are old-and-bold people.
Some pilots are old people.
Thus some old people are not old-and-bold people.

EIO-3   Valid

8.5 Enthymemes

Supply the probably missing proposition, put the argument into standard syllogistic form and then determine whether it's validity.

1. Don is despicable because he cheats.

    Missing premise: All persons who cheat are despicable. (1st order)

    [All persons who cheat are despicable persons.]
    (All) Don is a person who cheats.
    (All) Don is a person who is despicable.

    AAA-1   Valid (Unless the addition is completely unreasonable, it should try to make the argument valid.)

2. When foreign trade improves the economy improves and when the economy improves things are good for everyone.

    Missing: Thus when foreign trade improves things are good for everyone. (3rd order)

    All times when the economy improves are times that are good for everyone.
    All times when foreign trade improves are times when the economy improves.
    [Thus_All times when foreign trade improves are times that are good for everyone.]

    AAA-1   Valid

3. All members of ΓΟΟΔ fraternity have elevated social consciences. Thus Bob's sense of right and wrong in society is advanced.

    Missing: Bob is a member of ΓΟΟΔ fraternity. (2nd order)

    All members of ΓΟΟΔ fraternity are people with elevated social consciences.
    [(All) Bob is a member of ΓΟΟΔ fraternity.]
    Thus (All) Bob is a person with an elevated social conscience.

    AAA-1   Valid

4. Scientists study what interests them for only a fool ignores what interests him.

    Missing: No scientists are fools. (2nd order)

    All people who ignore what interests them are fools.
    [No scientists are fools.]
    Thus no scientists are people who ignore what interests them.

    AEE-2   Valid

8.6 Sorites

Restructure these sorites into chains of syllogisms.

1. No rational being enjoys the pain of others.
    Those who enjoy the pain of others are in need of counseling.
    <u>Many who are in need of counseling are denied it.</u>
    Thus some of those who are denied counseling are not rational.

    All those who enjoy the pain of others are in need of counseling.
    <u>Some who are in need of counseling are those who are denied it.</u>
    Thus some of those who enjoy the pain of others are denied counseling.

    No rational being is one of those who enjoy the pain of others.
    <u>Some of those who enjoy the pain of others are denied counseling.</u>
    Thus some of those who are denied counseling are not rational people.

2. Successful football players are violent.
    Pacifists are never violent.
    Brother Francisco is a pacifist.
    Thus he doesn't play football successfully.

    All successful football players are violent persons.
    <u>No pacifists are violent persons.</u>
    No pacifists are successful football players.

    No pacifists are successful football players.
    <u>(All) Brother Francisco is a pacifist.</u>
    Thus (No) Brother Francisco is a person who plays football successfully.

8.7 Disjunctive and Hypothetical Syllogisms

Identify the kind of syllogism offered and discuss its likely validity or invalidity.

1. Telemarketers are either desperate or duplicitous. This telemarketer is as honest as the day is long. She must, therefore, be desperate.

    Alternative syllogism. There's probably a bifurcation (black or white fallacy) here – even among telemarketers there are many motivations.

2. If God were all-powerful then He could make a stone so heavy He couldn't lift it. But if God could make a stone so heavy He couldn't lift it, then He wouldn't be all-powerful. Therefore if God were all-powerful He wouldn't be all-powerful.

    Hypothetical syllogism. This is a classic paradox. It's usually considered to be a logical error to try to attribute contradictory properties – here the ability to make the rock and the ability to lift it – to one situation.

3. If the erosion on the Sphinx and its enclosure were made by water then the figure must have been carved more than 12,500 years ago. Accepted Egyptology says it was carved by Khafre in about 2550 B.C.E. Thus the erosion must not be due to water.

    Hypothetical but mixed syllogism. What is here roughly is the Modus Tollens formal argument that will be discussed later.

8.8 The Dilemma

*Discuss the reasonability of these dilemmas,
offering counter dilemmas when appropriate.*

1. If things go well under the administration of the chair, then there seems no reason to have a chair; but if things do not go well under the administration of the chair, then there seems no reason to have a chair. Things must either go well or not. Thus there seems no reason to have a chair.

    You could try a counter dilemma involving an assumption about a chair's doing better than one could expect under trying circumstances, but it would probably be as shaky as the original. Analysis ought to suggest that closer examination of what the circumstances are and how the chair's efforts contributed to things going well or prevented things from being worse is needed.

2. If we win the conflict in Iraq then we will lose face [1st-rate industrial power defeats 3rd-rate underdeveloped power]; but if we don't win it then we will lose face [3rd-rate underdeveloped power overcomes 1st-rate industrial power]. We have to win or not, so we're doomed to lose face over Iraq.

    A similar argument by Senator George Akin (R-VT) was offered near the end of the Vietnam conflict. One might here argue that one could not "win" the fight and still preserve face, say, by turning management over to the Iraqis or the UN without forcing a "deciding battle."

3. In selecting a mate you either wind up with someone who makes you happy or someone who makes you sad. If your mate makes you happy then you have chosen successfully. If your mate makes you sad then you have learned a lesson which will allow you to choose more wisely later, so, in an odd sense, you have chosen successfully here, too. Thus any choice of a mate is in some way successful.

    Each "horn" of this dilemma is actually a hypothetical syllogism which is at least reasonable. There is, of course, the possibility that the second option won't come about because you will choose to avoid the risk of a second partnership (unless you see that as a form of "having chosen wisely").

9.2　The Symbols for Conjunction, Negation and Disjunction

Using the appropriate truth table definitions for the dot, wedge and curl, determine whether the statements are true or not.

1. George Washington was our first president $\cdot$ ~ Abraham Lincoln was our second.

    T $\cdot$ ~ F $=$ T $\cdot$ T $=$ T

2. ~Tijuana is the capital of Mexico $\vee$ Jerusalem is the capital of Egypt.

    ~ F $\vee$ F $=$ T $\vee$ F $=$ T

3. If Tijuana is not the capital of Mexico, then Stockholm is not the capital of Iraq.

    ~ F $\supset$ ~ F $=$ T $\supset$ T $=$ T

9.3　Conditional Statements and Material Implication

Assuming that A and B are true, X and Y are false, and the values of P and Q are not known, what can be determined about the following?

1. (P $\vee$ Q) $\supset$ [A $\cdot$ ~ (X $\cdot$ ~ Y)]

(? $\vee$?) $\supset$ [T $\cdot$ ~ (F $\cdot$ ~ F)]	True and anything is anything
(? $\vee$?) $\supset$ [~ (F $\cdot$ T)]	~ F $\equiv$ T
(? $\vee$?) $\supset$ ~ F	(F $\cdot$ T) $\equiv$ F
(? $\vee$?) $\supset$ T	as above
T	anything implying T is T

2. [P $\supset$ (Q $\vee$ X)] $\supset$ [(P $\supset$ Q) $\supset$ (P $\supset$ X)]

    [?$_1$ $\supset$ (?$_2$ $\vee$ F)] $\supset$ [(?$_1$ $\supset$?$_2$) $\supset$ (?$_1$ $\supset$ F)]

    [?$_1$ $\supset$?$_2$] $\supset$ [(?$_1$ $\supset$?$_2$) $\supset$ ~ ?$_1$]　$\Theta \vee$ F $= \Theta$ // $\Theta \supset$ F $=$ ~Θ

    (?$_1$ $\supset$?$_2$) $\supset$ ~ ?$_1$　　　$\Theta \supset$ ($\Theta \supset \Phi$) $= \Theta \supset \Phi$

    The value is <u>undetermined</u> because if ?$_1$ and ?$_2$ should both be true, the overall expression would be false, but otherwise true.

9.4　Some Common Argument Forms

Use truth tables to determine the validity or invalidity of the following arguments.

1. p $\supset$ (q $\cdot$ r)
    p $\supset$ ~ (q $\vee$ r)
    $\therefore$　~ p

    Here a slightly different approach looks at a statement form that is closely tied to the argument. Called the *Associated Statement Form*, it is created by combining all the premises by conjunction to generate a *Premise-set* and then setting it to imply the conclusion. It turns out that the *ASF* is tautologous when and only when the argument from which it was derived is valid. This allows us to check for validity slightly indirectly, but more formally.

			A	P 1	B	P 2	P set	C	A S F
p	q	r	q · r	p ⊃ A	q v r	~ B	P 1 · P 2	~ p	P set ⊃ C
T	T	T	T	T	T	F	F	F	T
T	T	F	F	F	T	F	F	F	T
T	F	T	F	F	T	F	F	F	T
T	F	F	F	F	F	T	F	F	T
F	T	T	T	T	T	F	F	T	T
F	T	F	F	T	T	F	F	T	T
F	F	T	F	T	T	F	F	T	T
F	F	F	F	T	F	T	T	T	T

Here you see that the ASF is a tautology, so the argument is valid.

2.   q

∴ [(p ⊃ q) ⊃ q] ⊃ q }

P 1		A	B	C		A S F
p	q	p ⊃ q	A ⊃ q	B ⊃ q	q	q ⊃ C
T	T	T	T	T	T	T
T	F	F	T	F	F	T
F	T	T	T	T	T	T
F	F	T	F	T	F	T

This one could be decided with a little thought. The only way for an argument to be proven invalid is for there to be a case where all the premises are true and the conclusion is false. Here the premise "p" has to be true. But it's also the consequent of the conclusion and, when the consequent of a conditional is true, the conditional is true. Thus, if the premiss is true the conclusion can't be false, so the argument is valid.

3. $p \supset (q \vee r)$
  $(q \cdot r) \supset s$
  $\therefore \ p \supset s$

				A	P 1	B	P 2	P set	C	A S F
p	q	r	s	q v r	p ⊃ A	q · r	B ⊃ s	P 1 · P 2	p ⊃ s	P set ⊃ C
T	T	T	T	T	T	T	T	T	T	T
T	T	T	F	T	T	T	F	F	F	T
T	T	F	T	T	T	F	T	T	T	T
T	T	F	F	T	T	F	T	T	F	F
T	F	T	T	T	T	F	T	T	T	T
T	F	T	F	T	T	F	T	T	F	T
T	F	F	T	F	F	F	T	F	T	T
T	F	F	F	F	F	F	T	F	F	F
F	T	T	T	T	T	T	T	T	T	T
F	T	T	F	T	T	T	F	F	T	T
F	T	F	T	T	T	F	T	T	T	T
F	T	F	F	T	T	F	T	T	T	T
F	F	T	T	T	T	F	T	T	T	T
F	F	T	F	T	T	F	T	T	T	T
F	F	F	T	F	T	F	T	T	T	T
F	F	F	F	F	T	F	T	T	T	T

This shows a 4-variable table, but it's done just as the shorter ones are. However, notice that in the ASF column the values in the 4th and 8th rows are "F." Any time the ASF is not a tautology, the related argument is invalid.

9.8 Statement Forms and Material Equivalence

Use truth tables to determine whether these are tautologies, self-contradictions or contingent.

1. $[P \cdot (\sim P \vee Q)] \supset Q$

P	Q	[P	·	(~	P	v	Q)]	⊃	Q
T	T	T			T	T			T
T	F	T			T	F			F
F	T	F			F	T			T
F	F	F			F	F			F

The table shows all combinations of values for P and Q.

P	Q	[P	·	(~	P	v	Q)]	⊃	Q
T	T	T		F	T	T			T
T	F	T		F	T	F			F
F	T	F		T	F	T			T
F	F	F		T	F	F			F

This table shows the "worked out value" for ~P and the source P column is reduced in size to make it easier to see what is active.

P	Q	[P	·	(~	P	v	Q)]	⊃	Q
T	T	T		F	T	T	T		T
T	F	T		F	T	F	F		F
F	T	F		T	F	T	T		T
F	F	F		T	F	T	F		F

The value for the wedge is developed; source columns shrink.

P	Q	[P	·	(~	P	v	Q)]	⊃	Q
T	T	T	T	F	T	T	T		T
T	F	T	F	F	T	F	F		F
F	T	F	F	T	F	T	T		T
F	F	F	F	T	F	T	F		F

The value for the dot is developed; source columns shrink.

P	Q	[P	·	(~	P	v	Q)]	⊃	Q
T	T	T	T	F	T	T	T	T	T
T	F	T	F	F	T	F	F	T	F
F	T	F	F	T	F	T	T	T	T
F	F	F	F	T	F	T	F	T	F

The final value for the expression is generated and shows this is a tautology.

2.   (~ P ⊃ ~ Q) v ~ (P ⊃ Q)

An alternative approach is to "build up" values from the inside out.

P	Q	~ P	~ Q	~ P ⊃ ~ Q	P ⊃ Q	~ (P ⊃ Q)	(~ P ⊃ ~ Q) v ~ (P ⊃ Q)
T	T	F	F	T	T	F	T
T	F	F	T	T	F	T	T
F	T	T	F	F	T	F	T
F	F	T	T	T	T	F	T

Again, since the last column is always true, this is a tautology.

3.   [P v (Q · R)] ≡ [(~ P ⊃ R) · ~ (~ P v ~ R)]

To make the table more compact, shortcut identifiers are assigned to columns. "A" is used to represent the column "Q · R ," "D" to represent " ~ P v ~ R ," and so on. The complex statement being evaluated is shortcutted in the column headed B ≡ F .

			A	B		C		D	E	F	
P	Q	R	Q · R	P v A	~ P	~ P ⊃ R	~ R	~ P v ~ R	~ D	C · E	B ≡ F
T	T	T	T	T	F	T	F	F	T	T	T
T	T	F	F	T	F	T	T	T	F	F	F
T	F	T	F	T	F	T	F	F	T	T	T
T	F	F	F	T	F	T	T	T	F	F	F
F	T	T	T	T	T	T	F	T	F	F	F
F	T	F	F	F	T	F	T	T	F	F	T
F	F	T	F	F	T	T	F	T	F	F	F
F	F	F	F	F	T	F	T	T	F	F	T

150

10.1 Formal Proof of Validity

Construct a formal proof of validity using the Rules of Inference. Be sure to indicate from which step(s) and by what rule you arrived at each step or your proof.

1. (P v Q) ⊃ (S · R)
    P · ~ T
    ∴ S

1.	(P v Q) ⊃ (S · R)	Premise
2.	P · ~ T	Premise / ∴ S
3.	P	2 , Simp
4.	P v Q	3 , Add
5.	S · R	1 , 4 , MP
6.	S	5 , Simp

2. (P ⊃ Q) v (~ P ⊃ R)
    P · ~ Q
    ~ Q · S
    ∴ R

1.	(P ⊃ Q) v (~ P ⊃ R)	Premise
2.	P · ~ Q	Premise
3.	~ Q · P	Premiss / ∴ R
4,	P	2 , Simp
5.	P v ~ P	4 , Add
6.	Q v R	1 , 5 , CD
7.	~ Q	3 , Simp
8.	R	6 , 7 , DS

There's a temptation to try to get ~Q from the second premise. While that isn't an unreasonable move, it doesn't fit within the rules we have – you can only simplify out the first conjunct. Later, however, you'll have the rule of commutation that allows you to "turn around" conjunctions (disjunctions, too).

10.2 The Rule of Replacement

Construct a formal proof of validity using both the Rules of Inference and those of Replacement. Be sure to indicate from which step(s) and by what rule you arrived at each step or your proof.

1. (P ⊃ Q) v (~ P ⊃ R)
    P · ~ Q
    ∴ R

1.	~ (P ⊃ Q) v (P ⊃ R)	Premise
2.	P · ~ Q	Premise / ∴ R
3.	P	2 , Simp
4.	P v ~ P	3 , Add
5.	Q v R	1 , 4 , CD
6.	~ Q · P	2 , Com
7.	~ Q	6 , Simp
8.	R	5 , 7 , DS

Note that this largely the same inference as in problem 2 (in the previous set). The difference is that, with access to the rule of commutation, you didn't need the third premise to get ~Q.

2. $\sim(P \cdot Q) \cdot (P \supset R)$
     $\underline{\sim(\sim P \vee \sim S)}$
     $R \cdot S$

```
1.  ~(P·Q)·(P⊃R)              Premise
2.  ~(~Pv~S)                  Premise/∴R·S
3.  (~Pv~Q)·(~PvR)           1, DeM
4.  ~Pv(~Q·R)                3, Dist
5.  P⊃(~Q·R)                 4, Impl
6.  ~~(P·S)                   2, DeM
7.  P·S                       6, DN
8.  P                         7, Simp
9.  S·P                       7, Com
10. S                         9, Simp
11. ~Q·R                      5,8,MP
12. R·~Q                      11, Com
13. R                         12, Simp
14. R·S                       13,10, Conj
```

There are several rather different paths that be taken here. Unless you're told there is a premium on brevity (or some other approach), none is any better than the others. One here is below.

```
1.   ~(P·Q)·(P⊃R)             Premise
2.   ~(~Pv~S)                 Premise/∴R·S
3.   (P⊃R)·~(P·Q)            1, Com
4.   P⊃R                      3, Simp
5.   ~~P·~~S                  2, DeM
6.   P·S                      5, DN
7.   S·P                      5, Com
8.   P                        6, Simp
9.   S                        7, Simp
10.  R                        4,8,MP
11.  R·S                      10,9, Conj
```

A little more brief but whether clearer or not is in the eye of the logician.

10.3 Proof of Invalidity

Prove the following invalid by the method os assigning values.

1. $P \supset (Q \vee R)$
     $(Q \cdot R) \supset S$
     $\therefore P \supset S$

When P and Q are true but R and S are false, the argument is shown invalid

2. $P \equiv \sim Q$
     $Q \equiv \sim R$
     $\underline{R \equiv P}$
     R

When P and R are both true and Q is false, the argument is shown invalid.

152

10.4 Inconsistency

Either construct a formal proof of validity or prove the argument invalid through the method of assigning values.

1. p ≡ (q · r) , (q v s) ⊃ t ⊢ ~ t ⊃ ~ p

1.	p ≡ (q · r)	premise
2.	(q v s) ⊃ t	premise / ∴ ~ t ⊃ ~ p
3.	[p ⊃ (q · r)] · [(q · r) ⊃ p]	1 , EQ
4.	p ⊃ (q · r)	3 , Simp
5.	~ p v (q · r)	4 , Impl
6.	(~ p v q) · (~ p v r)	5 , Dist
7.	~ p v q	6 , Simpl
8.	p ⊃ q	7 , Impl
9.	~ t ⊃ ~ (q v s)	2 , Trans
10.	~ ~ t v ~ (q v s)	9 , Impl
11.	~ ~ t v (~ q · ~ s)	10 , DeM
12.	(~ ~ t v ~ q) · (~ ~ t v ~ s)	11 , Dist
13.	~ ~ t v ~ q	12 , Simp
14.	~ t ⊃ ~ q	13 , Impl
15.	q ⊃ t	14 , Trans
16,	p ⊃ t	8 , 15 , HS
17.	~ t ⊃ ~ p	16 , Trans

2. p ⊃ q , r v ~ s , ~ (~ p · ~ r) ⊢ (p · q) v (r · s)

If p and s are both false, then the first two premises are true – false implies anything is true; not-false (i.e., true) or anything is true – and the conclusion is false. All that's needed is to find a way to have the third premise also true; if r is true, then premise three is true too. That means that the argument is invalid regardless of q's value.

10.5 Indirect Proof of Validity.

Construct in indirect proof of validity.

1. (p v ~ p) ⊃ (q · r) , (q ⊃ r) ⊢ r

1.	(p v ~ p) ⊃ (q · r)	Premise
2.	q ⊃ r	Premise / ∴ r
3.	~ r	IP assumption
4.	~ q	2 , 3 , MT
5.	~ q v ~ r	4 , Add
6.	~ (q · r)	5 , DeM
7.	~ (p v ~ p)	1 , 6 , MT
8.	~ p · ~ ~ p	7 , DeM
9.	r	IP from 8

Since step 8 is a contradiction which resulted from the assumption in step 3, step 9 must be the case.

10.6 Shorter Truth-Table Technique.

Show the following to be valid or invalid by the shorter truth-table method.

1. ~ (p · q) ⊃ ~ (r ∨ s) ⊦ r ∨ q

    Begin by assuming the premise is true and the conclusion false.

            ~ (p · q) ⊃ ~ (r ∨ s) ⊦ r ∨ q
                         T   F

    Work Out "forced values" then insert them where they fit.

            ~ (p · q) ⊃ ~ (r ∨ s) ⊦ r ∨ q
                         T   F
                                              F   F
                      F   F

    Work out the values that are forced from the earlier inferences.

            ~ (p · q) ⊃ ~ (r ∨ s) ⊦ r ∨ q
                         T   F
                                              F   F
                     F   F
                  F
            T
                              T
                                   F
                                      F

    Each line downward shows a new forced value. The ultimate
    result shows that when q, r, and s are all false, the premise is true
    and the conclusion is false. That means that the argument is
    invalid. (P's value makes no difference.)

2. p ⊃ ~ (q ∨ r) , ~ (q · r) ⊃ s ⊦ p ⊃ s

    Begin by assuming that the premises are true and the conclusion false.

    p ⊃ ~ (q ∨ r) , ~ (q · r) ⊃ s ⊦ p ⊃ s
      T   T   F

    Work out the forced values and insert them where appropriate.

    p ⊃ ~ (q ∨ r) , ~ (q · r) ⊃ s ⊦ p ⊃ s
      T   T   F
    T   F   T   F

    Continue working out forced values from earlier inferences.

    p ⊃ ~ (q ∨ r) , ~ (q · r) ⊃ s ⊦ p ⊃ s
      T   T   F
    T   F   T   F
          T   F
              F   T

154

All that's left is seeing that the false wedge (premise 1) means both q and r have to be false but that the true conjunction (premise 2) means they both have to be true. Since that obviously can't be the case, the assumption that the argument is invalid – i.e., that the premises are true and the conclusion false – must be wrong. If it's not invalid, then it must be valid. And, when using the shortened truth table method, discovering this sort of contradiction is the way you prove validity.

$$p \supset \sim (q \lor r), \sim (q \cdot r) \supset s \vdash p \supset s$$

```
p   ⊃   ~   (  q   v   r  ),   ~   (  q   •   r  )   ⊃   s   ⊦   p   ⊃   s
    T                                                    T           F
T                                                        F       T   F
        T                                                        T
                        F                                T
                    F                                T   T
                F       F                        T   T
```

11.4 Traditional Subject-Predicate Propositions

Translate each of the following into quantificational symbolism using the abbreviations suggested. Be sure not to begin with a "curl."

1. Both anarchists and democrats have high opinions of man. (Ax = x is an anarchist; Dx = x is a democrat; Hx = x has a high opinion of man.)

   It's often easiest to symbolize quantificational statements by first paraphrasing to come as close to standard categorical form as you can.

   All who are both anarchists and democrats are individuals who have a high opinion of man.

   Doing the symbolization in steps also lessens the chance of error.

   All who are both Ax and Dx are Hx.

   Insert the appropriate connectives.

   All who are (A x · D x) are P x.

   Since this is roughly the format of an A proposition, the full symbolization is

   (x)[(A x · D x) ⊃ P x]

2. To be permitted to play handball you have to be assigned locker space or not use the locker room. (Px = x is permitted to play handball; Ax = x is assigned locker space; Ux = x can use the locker room.)

   Start with the paraphrase.

   All who are permitted to play handball are either assigned locker space or not use the locker room.

   Insert the assigned abbreviations.

   All Px are either Ax or not Ux.

   Insert the appropriate connectives.

   All Px are (Ax v ~ Ux).

   Again this resembles an A proposition, so the full symbolization is

   (x)[Px ⊃ (Ax v ~Ux)]

11.5 Proving Validity

Construct a formal proof of validity for the following.

1. (x) (F x ⊃ G x)
   (∃ x) (H x · ~ G x)
   ∴ (∃ x) (H x · ~ F x)

1.	(x) (F x ⊃ G x)	Premise
2.	(∃ x) (H x · ~ G x)	Premise
3.	H a · ~ G a	2 , E I
4.	F a ⊃ G a	1 , U I
5.	H a	3 , Simp
6.	~ G a · H a	3 , Com
7.	~ G a	6 , Simp
8.	~ F a	4 , 7 , M T
9.	H a · ~ F a	5 , 8 , Conj
10.	(∃ x) (H x · ~ F x)	9 , E G

2. (x) (A x ⊃ B x)
   (x) (~ C x ⊃ ~ B x)
   (x) (A x ⊃ C x)

1.	(x) (A x ⊃ B x)	Premise
2.	(x) (~ C x ⊃ ~ B x)	Premise
3.	A a ⊃ B a	1 , U I
4.	~ C a ⊃ ~ B a	2 , U I
5.	B a ⊃ C a	4 , Trans
6.	A a ⊃ C a	3 , 5 , H S
7.	(x) (A x ⊃ C x)	6 , U G

11.6 Proving Invalidity

Prove the invalidity of the following arguments.

1. (x) (C x ⊃ A x)
   (x) (D x ⊃ A x)
   ∴ (x) (D x ⊃ C x)

Verbally this could be *All Cats are Animals, All Dogs are Animals, so All Dogs are Cats*, which is clearly invalid. The simplest assignment of values would be where a was a dog (and an animal) but not a cat.

C a ⊃ A a

D a ⊃ A a

D a ⊃ C a

C a	⊃	A a	D a	⊃	A a	D a	⊃	C a
F	T	T	T	T	T	T	F	F
	T			T			F	

2. $(\exists x)(Ix \cdot Tx)$
   $\underline{(\exists x)(Tx \cdot Ax)}$
   $\therefore (\exists x)(Ix \cdot Ax)$

Verbally this could be Some Iraqi are Terrorists, Some Terrorists are Addled, so Some Iraqi are Addled. The simplest evaluation would be with two individuals a and b, where a was Iraqi and terrorist but not addled and b was addled and terrorist but not Iraqi.

$(Ia \cdot Ta) v (Ib \cdot Tb)$
$\underline{(Ta \cdot Aa) v (Tb \cdot Ab)}$
$\therefore (Ia \cdot Aa) v (Ib \cdot Ab)$

Ia	·	Ta)	v	(Ib	·	Tb)	(Ta	·	Aa)	v	(Tb	·	Ab)	(Ia	·	Aa)	v	(Ib	·	Ab)
T		Ta)	F			Tb)	T		F	T			T	T		F	F			T
	T				F			T				T			F			F		
			T							**T**							**F**			

11.7 Asyllogistic Inference

Translate the following into quantificational notation using the suggested symbols.

1. Only players who were not club members were charged admission. (Px, Mx, Cx)

   Rewritten: All who were charged were both players and not members.

   $(x)[Cx \supset (Px \cdot {\sim}Mx)]$

2. Not all students who work hard get both good grades and a good job. (Sx, Wx, Gx, Jx)

   Rewritten: Some who are students and work hard are not both receivers of good grades and of a good job.

   $(\exists x)[(Sx \cdot Wx) \cdot {\sim}(Gx \cdot Jx)]$

12.2 Argument by Analogy

Determine whether the following analogies are arguments or not.

1. To be seventy years old is like climbing the Alps. You reach a snow-crowned summit, and see behind you the deep valley stretching miles and miles away, and before you other summits higher and whiter, which you may have strength to climb, or may not. Then you sit down and meditate and wonder which it will be. **Henry Wadsworth Longfellow** (1807–82), U.S. poet. Letter, 13 March 1877.

   As one might expect of a poet, the language beautifully creates a physical image and the emotions it evokes, but there's no argument. If there were, there would have to be some sort of conclusion argued to, but none is there.

157

2.	The role of religion in society has been to develop decency, honesty character and education for the betterment of humanity. Darrow said: "[Trade unions] have done more for decency, for honesty, for education, for the betterment of the race, for the developing of character in man, than any other association of men." From this we can infer that Darrow thought of trade unionism as a religion.
[**Clarence Darrow** (1857–1938), U.S. lawyer, writer. *The Railroad Trainman* (Nov. 1909).]

The conclusion *Darrow thought of trade unionism as a religion* is indicated by the indicating phrase *From this we can infer that....* The claimant is using the parallel workings of religion and trade unions as the basis for the analogical argument.

12.3 Appraising Analogical Arguments

1.	Determine what the analogy is and what it is arguing, then determine whether each of the added pieces of information (taken separately) makes the argument stronger or weaker, or makes no impact on it
Ruth and Keith have spent their summer vacation over the past decade traveling, visiting places they've never been before. They have always enjoyed their trips. They have decided to travel this year, too, and anticipate enjoying the trip.
   a.	Suppose that their annual travels had gone on for 20 years rather than 10.
   b.	Suppose that their travels had included the U.S., Europe, Asia and Africa.
   c.	Suppose they count their travels as among the highlights of their marriage.
   d.	Suppose that they had a baby six months ago and plan to take her along.
   e.	Suppose that Ruth has just completed her fourth one-woman art exhibit.
   f.	Suppose that they have always traveled in the spring and plan to do so again.

   a.	This increases the number of "entities," in this case the travels. (#1)

   b.	This shows increased variety of instances in the premises. (#2)

   c.	This is much stronger evidence than the conclusion asserts. (#6)

   d.	This shows a significant disanalogy with the earlier cases. (#5)

   e.	It's unlikely that this has any relevance (at least in terms of what has been shown here) to the argument. (#4)

   f.	This is an added similarity in the premises. (#3)

2.	Analyze the following argument in terms of the six criteria given, then argue whether it is a good argument or not.

Harry just purchased a new Ford pickup. It's Harry's third one. Among members of Harry's family they've owned 36 such Fords over the past 50 years. None of them has ever had a lemon. Harry plans to use his new vehicle in construction, just as Harry's family has always done. He needed this one because he drove the last one up the Al-Can Highway to Alaska, used it on the job for two years, and then sold it for more than he'd originally paid for it. Harry bought his first one as a ten-year-old used truck with 140,000 miles on it. It lasted another ten years in Texas heat. He figures this one was a pretty smart purchase.

1. The 36 trucks Harry's family has owned is, relative to personally-owned trucks, quite a large number of entities.

2. We know, at least, that Harry's trucks did well in Alaska and Texas. With 33 other Fords owned over a 50-year span, it's reasonable to infer there was a substantial variety of vehicles looked at.

3. Although all we're told is that the vehicles are all Fords and trucks, one could assume that trucks, especially those of one brand, would have a significant number of characteristics in common.

4. The behavior of the older trucks is likely to be relevant to that of the new pickup.

5. Although there surely are differences in trucks over half a century and in the large number of owner/drivers suspected, we're not told of any disanalogies that would cause difficulties.

6. Harry's conclusion that his pickup purchase is a smart one, that is certainly not an excessive inference.

Overall, since all the aspects of appraisal are positive, it's appropriate to infer that this is a pretty good argument.

12.4 Refutation by Logical Analogy

*Identify the argument being refuted and explain
whether the refuting analogy succeeds or not.*

Recent hypotheses have been advanced that the hatred we so much abhor in human behavior may be the result of genetic coding. The underlying data suggests that primitive humans were more likely to survive in groups than alone. Moreover, the argument runs, since different social groups (families, clans, tribes, etc.) were often in competition with each other for limited resources, developing antipathy toward other bands was a valuable survival characteristic. In time the thesis leads us to the position this developed into a genetic predisposition to hate anyone not in our "group." This makes as much sense as arguing that we all have a genetic predisposition to cannibalism. After all, there have been periods when limited availability of food made other people the easiest "crop." Looking at cases like the Donner Party or Alferd Packer show that cannibalism is a route to survival. So should we look on our neighbors as likely to eat us if they haven't made it to the store recently?

The argument is first that throughout human history devotion to one's own group has been a survival characteristic. Second it is claimed that hostility toward other groups is a significant element in devotion to one's own group. Not stated, but assumed, is the idea that personality traits which lead to survival tend to be selected for genetically. The conclusion, then, is that hostility toward other groups (dramatically called "hatred") has been encoded in human genetics.

The attempt to refute this argument is through a cannibalism analogy. The fact that cannibalism can, on occasion, be an aid to survival, it is probable that the act's occurrence is of rare importance. The "hatred" argument suggests that, in principle, it is generally useful. Overall, this is unlikely to be a good argument: the claimed analogy is too different from the original argument.

13.4 Methods of Causal Analysis

A.   The Method of Agreement

*Analyze the following inference, explaining how it is a case of the **Method of Agreement**. Discuss the limitations of this method in this attempt to determine causality.*

A young man entered college and was away from parental supervision for the first time in his life. In order to appear more sophisticated than he was, he went out drinking every weekend. On the first Saturday evening he went to Barney's and drank rum and cola. The next morning he had a terrible hangover. On the second Saturday he went to *The Golden Apple* and drank bourbon and cola. He awoke the following morning with a terrible hangover. On the third Saturday he went to a private party and drank vodka and cola. Subsequently he spent Sunday morning terribly hung-over. In the attempt to uncover the cause of his hangovers he looked at what had happened the night before the hangovers. It became clear that cola drinks cause them.

Pretty clearly this poor young man thinks he's using the Method of Agreement. In each of his Saturday night adventures the common element, he thinks, is the cola drink. Since each Saturday's party was at a different place and his other beverage seemed to change, yet each Sunday he was hung over, the sketch he worked out seemed to match the structure of this method. The problem with his inference, and one with this method in general, is that there was another commonality that wasn't obvious. In this case it was the fact that rum, bourbon and vodka all have significant alcohol content. If he were to repeat faithfully one of his Saturday escapades, but substitute some other mixing beverage for the cola, chances are he'd still wake up with a hangover. That would suggest that his cola-hypothesis had failed. The alcohol one, however, would still result from the more detailed analysis of the beverages.

B. The Method of Difference

*Analyze the following inference, explaining how it is a case of the **Method of Difference**. Discuss the limitations of this method in this attempt to determine causality.*

Steven and Stuart are identical twins. They graduated from Central High as co-valedictorians. They both decided to major in economics at State U. The Econ Department had a very rigid curriculum, virtually specifying what courses you would take and when you would take them, so they shared almost all their classes. However, Steven decided to join a fraternity while Stuart chose to live in the residence halls. Steven graduated in the top 10% of their class, received no appealing job offers, but was given a fellowship to a prestigious graduate school. Stuart graduated about the middle of their class, was not given an deal for grad school but was given a job with a high-status consulting firm. It's clear that the choice of living arrangements made the difference in their lives.

One of the reasons twins, not only of people, are very important in scientific research is their usefulness in studies like this. At first glance this does look like a quality case of the Method of Difference. So many characteristics here are shown to be common to them that the living arrangement difference stands out. The problem with this, and many real-world versions of this method, is that there are undoubtedly thousands of little elements that also differ between the two. They began accumulating when one was born first and they continued to accrue through their lives. The fraternity/residence hall difference is not simply one of living arrangements; it entails living near different people, participating in different activities, eating different foods, having different study procedures, and more other differences – both major and minor – than we can identify. What has happened here is that the analyst has selected the few features that she thought were noteworthy and based the inference on them. But, like most real-world cases, we'll never know whether there was some apparently minor element in the mix that made the real difference.

C. The Joint Method of Agreement and Difference

*Analyze the following inference, explaining how it is a case of the **Joint Method of Agreement and Difference**. Discuss the limitations of this method in this attempt to determine causality.*

A popular ad on '50s television featured school children running into their homes shouting: "Look, Ma, no cavities!" The ads would go on to explain that, for example, two classes of the same grade within the same elementary school had been selected to test "...the effectiveness of Fluoristan (stannous fluoride) in a program of properly-applied oral hygiene and professional dental care." One of the classes was given toothpaste with the Fluoristan, the other the same toothpaste without it. At the end of a testing period, usually six months to a year, the children would be checked to determine how many dental caries they had developed. At least according to the ads, the children exposed to Fluoristan averaged two or three fewer caries than the ones not so treated. The conclusion the toothpaste company hoped was evident to the viewer was that the Fluoristan was the key to preventing cavities.

Like most cases of the Joint Method of Agreement and Difference, there's a good deal of supposing here. What has happened is that the toothpaste researchers have (probably, if they're doing their work carefully) divided the school classes so that the kinds of children – race, gender, economic status, whatever – are pretty well mirrored in the two groups. The basic tooth-care protocol is the same within the two groups, the only significant difference being whether there is Fluoristan in their dentifrice. The investigators then analyze each group and, we suppose, find that the group with it have some average number of caries within the research period. They also find that the group without it presumably has a notably larger average number of caries. They use the Method of Agreement to infer that the Fluoristan group gets caries at a rate of x and to infer that the other group gets them at an $x+y$ rate. They then suppose that the two groups are, for all practical purposes, "identical" except for the use of the chemical. That use, then, becomes the difference element causing the fewer cavities. Although this experiment probably did identify an important tool in protecting teeth, the argument has all the same sorts of potential problems that each of the methods had separately.

D.   The Method of Residues

*Analyze the following inference, explaining how it is a case of the **Method of Residues**. Discuss the limitations of this method in this attempt to determine causality.*

Archimedes was given the assignment of determining whether the goldsmith who had constructed the king's crown had substituted base metals inside the crown for the gold he'd been given with which to make it. The king's stipulation, however, was that it was not to be damaged. The solution, according to legend, was that while getting into his bathtub he watched the water rise and intuited what would be known as Archimedes' Law. He filled a spouted pitcher to the brim with water, immersed the crown slowly, and caught the overflow. He then measured the volume of water forced out and repeated the experiment with the same volume of gold known to be pure. When he weighed the crown and the same-volume gold he saw that the crown was substantially lighted. From this he inferred that the crown had been adulterated, that the difference in weight resulted from some volume of the gold having been replaced by a lighter, less valuable metal.

This is one of the classic cases cited as a use of the Method of Residues. All the elements in the test remain constant except the crown and the same-volume gold. When the crown weighs than the gold what we have is a left-over effect (i.e., a residue). Like many uses of this method we are then sent back to discover a previously undiscovered difference in the experimental setup. Here the decision is that the goldsmith was a thief. In such inferences there are other options that may be overlooked – in this case perhaps there are enclosed spaces within the crown, ones which increase the volume but not the weight. Or what if the goldsmith had been clever enough to use a mix of two metals whose total weight/volume measurement matched the gold? Then Archimedes would have incorrectly declared the crown to be pure gold. As the earlier arguments suggested, the world may be substantially more complicated than Mill's Methods assume it is.

E.   The Method of Concomitant Variation

*Analyze the following inference, explaining how it is a case of the **Method of Concomitant Variation**. Discuss the limitations of this method in this attempt to determine causality.*

In the early 20th century women's hemlines were at the ankle and the economy was in a recession. By the late 20's flapper hemlines were above the knee and the stock market boomed. By the 30's hemlines had dropped to lower calf and we were in The Great Depression. Following WW II, hemlines again rose above the knee and the economy surged. In the 50's poodle skirts at mid-calf were the rage and the Eisenhower administration said we were in a "rolling recession." The 60's saw the popularity of the Mini and the Micro-Mini and the Dow Jones Industrials breaking 1000 for the first time in history. The Midi and Maxi appeared in the 70's and the economy tanked. Since then there has been a wide variety of "accepted" hemlines – from very brief to ankle-length – and the economy has bounced all over. It's clear that, if women had any sense of patriotism, they'd all go out and shorten their skirts!

Although this looks something like the Method of Concomitant Variation, its conclusion is ridiculous. While it does seem historically true that hemlines and the economy rose and fell roughly in parallel, we'd need a lot more study to show why they would be related. In a case like this our intuitions might suggest that we have the cause-effect identification backward, that fluctuations in the economy are the causal factor. But wouldn't it seem more likely that in a bad economy we'd want to invest less fabric, not more, in clothing as a way to save money? In this argument, too, we need to be much more specific about timelines, looking to see which actually came first, the change in clothing or the one in the economy. [In this case the facts suggest that the economy varied first.] Why then the counterintuitive detail of hems dropping when the market does? Psychologists would probably tell us it has to do with the need to feel more protected (covered) when we feel economically insecure.

A harder case would have been had we mapped hemlines and the rate of long distance telephone use. They rise and fall together and in a far closer time frame. But they point to another limitation of this method; they're almost certainly both effects of the same cause – the economy. And sometimes numeric similarities are just coincidences.

14.5 Seven Stages of Scientific Discovery

Analyze the following in terms of the seven steps from this section.

One of the most puzzling phenomena in the history of humanity is the strange case of "villages that went mad." Their most frequent occurrences were in the Middle Ages, but there have been incidents as recently as 1976.

The first recorded case happened during the early fall of 1432 in the village of Ste. Gertrude in Germany. A traveler found everyone in the village over the age of about one year dead. There was food on the tables, partially eaten; there were no signs of invaders; and there were evidences of pairs of people having literally beaten, choked or stabbed each other to death. Some had clearly leapt from high windows or walked in the nearby river to drown. All had died, whether rich or poor. The traveler wrote: "From the banker's table with its white bread and broiled dove to the miller's with its hard rolls and cheese to the serf's with its black bread and onion soup, all sat empty as if the guests had merely excused themselves for a moment."

A second case happened in the French town of Villiers in the early fall of 1487. A priest reported coming out of his cell where he had been fasting to find all his parishioners at each other's throats, "…screaming madly and obscenely as if possessed by the Devil. And I knew that the Evil One had been present that day, for the aroma of the village baker's fresh loaves had driven me out with the intention of breaking my vow of hunger."

Dozens of other cases are reported, the last of which was the township of Stuart, Manitoba on October 3, 1976. The local RCMP constable (Mountie) was reporting to his superior in Winnipeg by radio, chatting about the church social he had just attended where he had gorged on the mayor's wife's special baked chicken and the pastor's wife's home-made French bread. Suddenly he began screaming about the "…green snakes that are coming out of the microphone." He evidently tore the mike from the console, rushed into the street and was killed trying to beat a moving semi-trailer truck to death with the mike. The driver, when questioned by the Mounties, said that "he ran right in front of the speeding vehicle, pounding and screaming as he was drawn under the wheels. By the time I stopped, he was crushed and dozens of others were outside screaming and attacking anything that moved. I sealed myself up in the cab, called for help on my CB and watched as men, women and children madly killed each other. It was like a scene from Hell."

The problem, clearly, is to figure out what caused people in so many places and times, to "go mad." **(1)** The initial hypothesis was that the cause had been something in Stuart's environment. **(2)**

164

Investigators in this case went to the Mounties' analysis of the "scene of the episode" in Stuart. They had taken samples from the town's water, atmosphere, and soil. They took biological samples from the victims. They also sampled foods that were on the tables and in the larders of the citizens. **(3)**

We might hypothesize, using Mill's Method of Agreement, that the cause of the madness was related to eating the bread, a common element in all the cases. Looking at specific data from the Mounties' investigation, we do find that both the affected people and the bread in their larders were infected with ergot, a by-product of the *Claviceps* fungus on rye. This lead scientists to hypothesize that, since bread in general is not problematic for people, the ergot might be the crucial element. **(4)**

If this hypothesis was correct, then feeding test animals bread infected with ergot ought to result in their exhibiting "madness" much as happened to the people of the several villages. **(5)** That result did occur among most of the animals. **(6)**

Further reflection on the data and results suggests that another relevant datum is that all the cases of so-called madness occurred in small, rural communities. It was either known or reasonably suspected that the flour used in the bread came from the local mill, often made into bread by the local baker. The recommendation is thus made that rye and rye flour ought to be examined carefully for the *Claviceps* fungus and, should it be there, be discarded. **(7)**

14.8 Classification as Hypothesis

What data are to be explained? What hypotheses are proposed to explain them? Evaluate the hypotheses in terms of the criteria that are detailed in section 14.3.

Recently there has been a major disturbance in the small Missouri town of Dixon. Children in the elementary school have been breaking out with severe rashes and terrible itching. It began with one 4th grader and quickly seemed to spread to most of the children in the school. The outbreak has not evidenced itself in any other school within a reasonable radius. School administrators have announced at least three times that they have "discovered" the answer to the disease. First they claimed it was an allergic reaction to bird droppings in the ceilings of the school. They closed the building, cleaned out the ceilings, and reopened classes. Children still itched. They said it was a new cleaner used on desks. They changed cleaners. Children still itched. They got a report from a doctor who said it was a "mass sociogenic illness," that is, they just convinced themselves they had it. Children still itched. One area mother suspected an attack by a small mite, driven from its usual hosts by spring rains. She treated her children and others with a natural insecticide, a club resin. None of those children now itch. It is thus clear that the mite is the true culprit in this case.

The phenomena to be explained are the uncontrollable itching and severe rashes of the children in the Dixon elementary school.

The first hypothesis was allergy to bird droppings in the school's ceilings. This was "tested" by closing school and thoroughly cleaning the school's ceilings. The children still itched. The hypothesis was wrong.

The second hypothesis was that the itching and rashes were due to the use on the desks of a new cleaner. They changed cleaners. The children still itched. The hypothesis was wrong.

A doctor suggested that it was a "mass sociogenic illness," meaning that it was all in the children's' imaginations. Although it's not stated in this passage, that claim resulted the children's being counseled that there was no real problem. The children still itched. The hypothesis was wrong.

One mother hypothesized that a near-invisible mite driven from its usual hosts by unusual rains had attacked the children. She applied a cube resin ("natural" insecticide) to several children. The itching stopped. The hypothesis was confirmed.

All of the hypotheses were consistent with accepted science **(1)** They all would have explained the illnesses had they been confirmed by experience **(2)**. All but the sociogenic illness were reasonably simple – how a large group of elementary schoolers would have all imagined matching symptoms seems rather complex **(3)**.

15. The Probability of Joint Occurrences

1. What is the probability of being dealt a flush? [5 cards, one suit]

    Any card is OK for the first one drawn/dealt. After that the remaining cards must all be the same suit as was the first one. You begin with 52 cards, 13 of each suit. With each card drawn/dealt you have one less in the deck and one less in the specific suit. $\frac{52}{52} \times \frac{12}{51} \times \frac{11}{50} \times \frac{10}{49} \times \frac{9}{48}$ There's really no point in working out the arithmetic. In fact it's actually easier to discover errors if the arithmetic is not worked out.

2. If five horses are running a race and are exactly evenly matched, but there are no ties, what is the probability that you will pick the first two horses (not necessarily in order) to finish the race?

    It's often useful to restate the problem in terms of the sequence of actions necessary to successfully do what the problem asks. In this case, in order to succeed, the first choice you make must be one of the first two finishers – two chances out of five. Your second choice must be the remaining top-2 finisher of the remaining four horses. $\frac{2}{5} \times \frac{1}{4}$

3. What is the probability of rolling all six numbers in six rolls of a die?

To do this you can roll any number the first time, one of the five remaining the second time and so on until you roll the last remaining number of the six . $\frac{6}{6} \times \frac{5}{6} \times \frac{4}{6} \times \frac{3}{6} \times \frac{2}{6} \times \frac{1}{6}$

4. If you have a 1/10 chance of failing each of your six classes, what is the probability of your failing at least one?

The only way you can not succeed in failing at least one class is to pass them all. If you have a 1/10 chance of failing a class then you have a 9/10 chance of passing the class. If you're to pass them all, the probability is $\frac{9}{10} \times \frac{9}{10} \times \frac{9}{10} \times \frac{9}{10} \times \frac{9}{10} \times \frac{9}{10}$. The probability of failing at least one is the complement of passing them all, or 1- p(pass all). $1 - \frac{9}{10} \times \frac{9}{10} \times \frac{9}{10} \times \frac{9}{10} \times \frac{9}{10} \times \frac{9}{10}$.

15.4 Probability of Alternative Occurrences

1. What is the probability of rolling a fair die and getting a number divisible by either 2 or 3?

This can be solved several ways. Least complicated is to list the possible outcomes then identify the ones that satisfy the problem's conditions. In this case you could roll a 1, 2, 3, 4, 5, or 6. 2, 4, and 6 are divisible by 2; 3 and 6 are divisible by 3. Thus the "successes" are 2, 3, 4, and 6. 1 and 5 are "failures." The answer, then, is 4/6.

The second way to solve the problem would be through use of the Alternative Theorem. In this case the probability of getting a number divisible by 2 is 3/6, the probability of getting a number divisible by 3 but not by 2 is 1/6 [that of one divisible by 3 is 2/6, but 6 is divisible by both 2 and 3, so has already been "counted"]. The Theorem can be interpreted either as $\frac{3}{6} + \frac{1}{6}$ or as

$\frac{3}{6} + \frac{2}{6} - \frac{1}{6}$.

2. If you hold 3 of a kind and 2 odd cards in a game of draw poker, are you more likely to better your hand by discarding the 2 and drawing or by holding the 3 of a kind and one of the two and drawing only one? Why?

The possibilities can be examined by showing all possible results.

X	X	X	Y	Z	Original deal				X	X	X	Y	Z	
X	X	X	X	A	1/47x46/46	=	46/47x46		X	X	X	Y	X	1/46
X	X	X	Y	X	3/47x1/46	=	3/47x46		X	X	X	Y	Y	2/46
X	X	X	Y	Y	3/47x2/46	=	6/47x46							
X	X	X	Z	X	3/47x1/46	=	3/47x46							
X	X	X	Z	Z	3/47x2/46	=	6/47x46							
X	X	X	N	X	40/47x1/46	=	40/47x46							
X	X	X	N	N	40/47x3/46	=	120/47x46							

3/46

184/47x46   141/47X46

If you keep only the 3 of a kind, the 7 ways you can improve your hand are shown on the left. The probability of each event is to the right, resolved to a common denominator in the middle column. It's summed at the bottom since these are all exclusive events. If you keep 3 of a kind and one more, the only way to improve your hand is either to get the 4th X or a second Y. To be able to compare the results, you need to get a matching denominator. The easiest way to get this is to multiply both numerator and denominator by 47. When both results have the same denominator we can compare numerators as a gauge of relative probability. Here tossing two cards gives you 184 chances of success (of the 47x46 total possibilities) while pitching one gives you only 141 chances. This means that you have more than a 20% better chance by discarding two cards.

15.5 Expectation Value

1. Assume that you have $1000 to invest. Your broker suggests two stocks, a blue chip and an aggressive one. Based on her experience she tells you that the blue chip has an 87% chance of being worth $1150 in a month but a 13% chance of being worth only $900 then, while the aggressive one has a 57% chance of being worth $1640 in a month and a 43% chance of being worth only $600. Which, based on expectation, is the better investment?

With the blue chip stock there is an 87% chance of the investment being worth $1150 and a 13% chance of being worth $900. Investment in it, then, has an expectation of ($1150 x .87) + ($900 x .13) = $1,117.50.

With the aggressive stock there is a 57% chance of the investment being worth $1640 and a 43% chance of its being worth $600. Investment in it, then, has an expectation of ($1640 x .57) + ($600 x .43) = $1,192.80.

Since the aggressive stock has an expected value of $75.30 more than the blue chip it is, *if* you're investing strictly on expectation, then the aggressive stock is the better investment. The problem with this decision, like all gambling (and playing the market **is** gambling), is that the blue chip has a much greater likelihood of preserving your nest egg.

2. Assume that you've been given a chance to play a new card game that costs differing amounts to play. You're allowed to cut a standard 52-card deck. You may pay $5 to pick a suit. If you cut that suit, you get $12. You may pay $3 to pick 2 denominations (like Q & K). If you cut that denomination, you get $14. You may pay $2 to pick a single denomination. Cutting correctly gives you $21. Or you can pay $1 to cut a specific card for a payoff of $50. Which is your best bet, based on expectation?

On the suit cut there's a ¼ chance of getting the suit, so the expectation is (1/4 x $12) = $3 (on a $5 play). Not too good.

On the 2 denomination cut there's an 8/52 chance, so the expectation is (8/52 x $14) = $2.15 on a $3 bet. Better, but not too good.

On the single denomination cut there's a 4/52 chance, so the expectation is (4/52 x $21) = $1.61 on a $2. So-so.

And the single card cut has a 1/52 chance and an expectation is (1/52 x $50) = 96¢ on a $1 bet. This one's the best chance of the plays.